The Rough Guide to

THE
LOST
SYMBOL

AN UNAUTHORIZED GUIDE

ROUGH
GUIDES

www.roughguides.com

Credits

The Rough Guide to The Lost Symbol
Additional contribution: J.D. Dickey
Picture Research: Andrew Lockett
Cartography: Katie Lloyd-Jones
Cover design: Tom Cabot
Production: Rebecca Short

Rough Guides Reference
Director: Andrew Lockett
Editors: Kate Berens, Peter Buckley,
Tracy Hopkins, Matthew Milton,
Joe Staines, Ruth Tidball

Publishing Information

This first edition published December 2009 by
Rough Guides Ltd, 80 Strand, London, WC2R 0RL
375 Hudson Street, New York 10014, USA
Email: mail@roughguides.com

Distributed by the Penguin Group:
Penguin Books Ltd, 80 Strand, London, WC2R 0RL
Penguin Group (USA), 375 Hudson Street, NY 10014, USA
Penguin Group (Australia), 250 Camberwell Road, Camberwell, Victoria 3124, Australia
Penguin Group (Canada), 90 Eglinton Avenue East, Suite 700, Toronto, Ontario, Canada M4P 2Y3
Penguin Group (New Zealand), Cnr Rosedale and Airborne Roads, Albany, Auckland, New Zealand

Typeset in Optima, Metaplus and Garamond to an original design by Dan May.
Printed in Italy by Legoprint S.p.A and in the USA by Lake Books.

256pp; includes index

A catalogue record for this book is available from the British Library.

ISBN: 978-1-84836-009-9

1 3 5 7 9 8 6 4 2

The Rough Guide to

THE
LOST
SYMBOL

Michael Haag

www.roughguides.com

Dedicated to
James and Lyn Davidson
friends and adepts

ABOUT THE AUTHOR

Michael Haag, who lives in London, is the author of several books of history, travel, biography and literary studies. These include *Alexandria: City of Memory* (Yale University Press), *The Templars: History and Myth, from Solomon's Temple to the Freemasons* (Profile Books, London, and Harper Collins, New York), *The Rough Guide to The Da Vinci Code* and *The Rough Guide to Tutankhamun*. You can visit Michael Haag's website at www.michaelhaag.com.

Contents

Basics

Context

Locations

Author

Introduction

'... a catalyst that would inspire mankind to rediscover the knowledge he had lost, empowering him beyond all imagination.'

THE LOST SYMBOL [CHAPTER 14]

The themes of knowledge lost and of the need for an almost alchemical transformation of mankind's outlook on the world run throughout *The Lost Symbol*. Only then can man become a god and take full responsibility for his destiny. That is the startling argument that Dan Brown puts forward in his latest thriller – a thriller that sometimes reads like a sacred quest.

The Lost Symbol is a gently stated but nevertheless audacious attack on the assumptions underlying Western civilization. It goes beyond even the challenge of *The Da Vinci Code*, in which Dan Brown argued that our modern understanding of history is based upon the deliberate suppression of an ancient truth. There he was questioning the pillar of Christian faith. In *The Lost Symbol* he says that our culture is suffering from a lack of wholeness brought about by two competing world views, one giving primacy to doctrinal faith, the other to pure rationality. Dan Brown says there is a third component to Western culture, one that has been long buried and ignored. It is the Ancient Mysteries which combined the material with the spiritual, the rational with faith, and which revealed that man and God were one.

The thrilling adventures of Robert Langdon through the twelve hours of the Washington night are that journey of transformation. Along the way Dan Brown tells the story of the Freemasons, of the Founding Fathers, of adepts like Albrecht Dürer and Sir Isaac Newton, and of their role in ensuring that the lost symbol is never really lost and is there to be rediscovered and realized today.

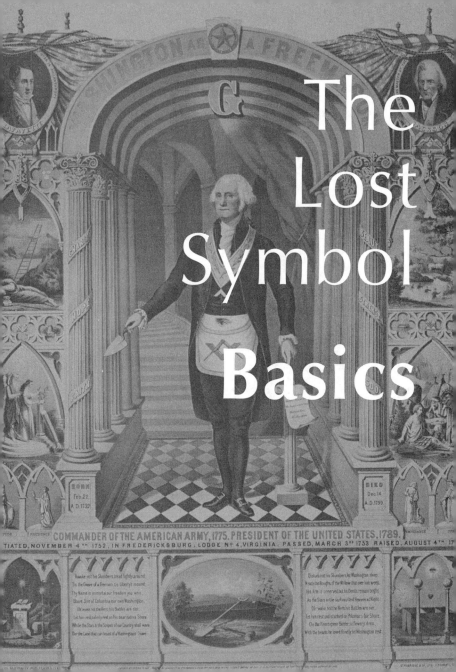

The Lost Symbol

Basics

What The Lost Symbol Says

AND WHAT ARE THE SECRET SOURCES?

'The famous Hermetic aphorism – *Know ye not that ye are gods?* – was one of the pillars of the Ancient Mysteries. As above, so below ... Man created in God's image ... Apotheosis. This persistent message of man's own divinity – of his hidden potential – was *the* recurring theme in the ancient texts of countless traditions. Even the Holy Bible cried out in Psalms 82:6: *Ye are gods!'*

THE LOST SYMBOL [CHAPTER 82]

At the heart of Dan Brown's *The Lost Symbol* is the quest for the Ancient Mysteries, that body of Graeco-Roman and ancient Egyptian knowledge that has the power to transform mankind. The Ancient Mysteries have been hidden, distorted or suppressed, though something of their meaning has been kept alive throughout the ages by adepts like the Renaissance artist Albrecht Dürer and the Enlightenment scientist Sir Isaac Newton, by America's Founding Fathers and by the Freemasons. Today the Ancient Mysteries are finding a new expression in noetic science, which includes the study of collective consciousness and the power of thought over matter; all of us are capable together of remaking the world around us, raising our lives to a higher plane. Mankind is on the verge of realizing itself as divine, each of us as gods.

But there are demons among the angels, and the danger is that the Ancient Mysteries will fall into the hands of Mal'akh, a crazed and demonic figure, the incarnation of everything evil and repressive, whose aim is to destroy the hopes of mankind. The Ancient Mysteries are 'out there somewhere' in Washington, DC, buried beneath an ancient portal, and Mal'akh has lured the Harvard symbologist Robert Langdon to show him the way. In the course of Dan Brown's fast-moving thriller, startling twists and turns of plot reveal unsuspected secrets about history, art and science, about places, politics and people in what the novel calls 'the Mystic City'.

As usual, Dan Brown has created his novel from a fusion of fact and fiction. 'Fact: All organizations in this novel exist … All rituals, science, artwork and monuments in this novel are real.' From these facts he develops his argument that by throwing off the shackles of corrupted faith, by linking science with ancient mysticism, by embracing the aims of America's Founding Fathers, of Freemasonry and of noetic science, we can arrive at 'the great promise of man becoming God'. But where do you draw the line between fact and fiction in *The Lost Symbol*? And are the 'facts' true? Is Dan Brown really Mal'akh in disguise, as some Christians would say? Or is he reworking that perennial story known to the ancient Egyptians as the Amduat, the journey through the twelve hours of the night until the soul is reborn again with the rising sun?

Dan Brown's Plot

It is sundown as Robert Langdon, Professor of Symbology at Harvard, flies into Washington, DC, lured by an urgent summons from his old friend Peter Solomon, head of the Smithsonian Institution who is also a Freemason of the Thirty-third Degree. The guest speaker at the Smithsonian's VIP dinner at the Capitol Building's Statuary Hall that evening has fallen ill, and Langdon

'Has the lecture been moved to a different room?' Langdon receives the first of many shocks when he speaks to Mal'akh on his cell phone in an empty Statuary Hall.

agrees to take his place. But Langdon arrives to find that the hall is empty, and when he phones Solomon's number a mysterious voice tells him, 'You are here, Mr Langdon, because I want you here', and that if he wants to see Solomon alive again he must lead the way to the portal that reveals the Ancient Mysteries, buried somewhere in the city. A moment later there is a scream from the nearby Rotunda. Solomon's severed right hand, newly tattooed with occult symbols, has been stuck on a spike and points mockingly upwards at the fresco in the dome, *The Apotheosis of George Washington*.

The mysterious voice belongs to Mal'akh; his name means 'angel', but as Mal'akh observes, angels and demons can be the same thing. Both can have their spiritual aspirations. 'I am magnificent', Mal'akh says, admiring his tattooed body in the mirror, his feet marked with the talons of a hawk, his legs patterned like Boaz and Jachin (the columns flanking Solomon's Temple), his pelvis an arch, his chest a double-headed phoenix. It's an ascending order of ancient and Masonic symbols reaching towards the godhead – quite literally in fact, as he has kept the very top of his head free for his final tattoo, the one he will apply tonight when he has forced Langdon to help him find the lost symbol. Preparing for this night, he listens to a favourite piece of music, Verdi's *Lux Aeternae*. But Mal'akh is the perversion of eternal light; he is a force of darkness – Lucifer incarnate. 'I am a masterpiece', he says, as he performs a series of rituals to prepare himself for the ultimate immolation.

Mal'akh wants to destroy Solomon. He wants to destroy the Freemasons and those powerful people who are its secret members. But his ambitions reach far beyond that. Solomon's sister Katherine has been making great advances in the field of noetic science and Mal'akh wants to destroy her too, obliterating all her work and thus wreck the hopes of mankind to transform itself, to combine Ancient Wisdom with modern science to raise itself to another plane.

The hand, the tattoos, the fresco, the Rotunda itself – all of these are clues towards understanding the mysteries confronting Langdon. And there is also the Masonic Pyramid he is carrying in his shoulder bag, a talisman that Solomon had asked him to protect. Within minutes of arriving at the Capitol Building, Langdon's world has turned upside down; everything has suddenly veered out of control. Bewildered and confused, Langdon finds himself immersed in a world of symbols, signs and myths that he frantically tries to piece together to create a new order out of chaos – and to find the answer to the quest, the secret that will win the release of his friend Peter Solomon.

But Langdon's mission becomes further complicated by the arrival at the Capitol of Inoue Sato, director of the CIA's Office of Security. She claims to have information that Mal'akh possesses the means to inflict terrible damage to national security, a crisis whose ramifications 'will be felt all around the world'. Sato has no interest in saving Peter Solomon; her objective is to use Langdon to lead her to Mal'akh. When Langdon forcibly escapes Sato so he can decode the symbols and reach Mal'akh to win the release of Solomon, he not only risks becoming Mal'akh's victim but he also becomes the quarry of the CIA.

Joined by Katherine Solomon, who has only narrowly avoided being murdered by Mal'akh in her lab, Langdon races through tunnels and the metro below the streets of Washington. He finds temporary sanctuary at the National Cathedral, where the disillusioned dean laments how the name of Jesus has been hijacked by causes throughout history, whether the Crusades, the Inquisition or the power struggles of American politics. But the dean is also a Freemason and he guides Langdon closer to an answer to the puzzle of the symbols that will lead to the secret portal and its

Ancient Mysteries. In his excitement at being at the threshold of the final answer, Langdon falls into a trap set by Mal'akh who, with the solution to the mystery in his hands goes off to what he imagines will be his own triumphal apotheosis, abandoning Katherine and Langdon to suffer slow and horrific deaths.

Yet in the end the hope remains that light will prevail over darkness. The twelve hours of night have passed and the sun is rising over the Mystical City as Langdon surveys a world reborn. He thinks of Katherine's belief that everything is about to change, and of her brother's faith that a new age of enlightenment is about to begin. 'And he thought of the words of a great prophet who had boldly declared: *Nothing is hidden that will not be made known; nothing is secret that will not come to light.*'

Journey Through the Mystical City: The Twelve Hours of Night

The action in Dan Brown's two other novels featuring Robert Langdon, *Angels and Demons* and *The Da Vinci Code*, takes place over the course of 24 hours. But, significantly, in *The Lost Symbol* the action covers only twelve hours – from sunset to dawn, the twelve hours of night. 'Outside the window the sun had set, but Langdon could still make out the slender silhouette of the world's largest obelisk' – this is Langdon flying into Washington DC in chapter 1 of the book. And in the Epilogue, Langdon is watching the sunrise over the city: 'A tiny speck of golden sunlight was glinting off the highest tip of the towering obelisk. The shining pinpoint grew quickly brighter, more radiant, gleaming on the capstone's aluminum peak. Langdon watched in wonder as the light transformed into a beacon that hovered above the shadowed city'.

Dan Brown deliberately placed the action of *The Lost Symbol* within the twelve hours of night, for those are the hours of the

The ancient in the modern world. The Washington National Monument obelisk in the midst of a recent security alert.

Amduat, the part of the ancient Egyptian Book of the Dead that serves as an hour-by-hour guide for navigating the dark night of the underworld, filled with deities, demons and monsters, before being reborn in the morning with the rising sun. Apart from anything else, *The Lost Symbol* is a spiritual journey, a voyage through darkness into light – and it all takes place within, and below, the mystical city.

Looking down Pennsylvania Avenue towards the Capitol building. Washington at night is the underworld which Langdon has to navigate.

THE MYSTICAL CITY

Washington, DC, is barely two hundred years old, but as Dan Brown points out it is filled with references to antiquity. According to *The Lost Symbol*, the Lincoln Memorial was 'inspired by the Parthenon' in Athens; the Jefferson Memorial was modelled on the

Pantheon in Rome; the Rotunda of the Capitol Building, it says, is a copy of Rome's Temple of Vesta and its dome is modelled on that of St Peter's Cathedral in the Vatican. The House of the Temple, headquarters of the Scottish Rite Freemasons, Southern Jurisdiction, is a replica of the 'temple of King Mausolus' at Halicarnassus in Asia Minor and is described as the Pantheon with a pyramid on top.

Moreover, says *The Lost Symbol*, 'the forefathers who founded this capital city first named her "Rome". They had named her river the Tiber and erected a classical capital of pantheons and temples', which they adorned with sculptures and paintings of Venus, Minerva, Apollo, Helios, Vulcan and Jupiter. As a tribute to the ancient world they erected an Egyptian obelisk, 'proclaiming thanks and honor to the demigod forefather for whom this capital city took its newer name. Washington.'

Not all of that is entirely accurate, despite Dan Brown's notice of 'Fact' at the front of his novel. More will be said about that elsewhere in this book. But what is relevant here is the impression Brown is trying to create of a city whose conceptual and spiritual roots go back to the ancient past. 'Even from the air, Washington, DC, exuded an almost mystical power', writes Brown in chapter 1, describing Langdon's view of the city as he flies in from Boston. And we are told in chapter 20 that at Harvard Langdon had lectured on 'the mystical symbolism of Washington, DC'. The same sense of spiritual communion inhabits the breast of the demoniacal Mal'akh, who, in chapter 2, after admiring his naked tattooed body, looks out upon the city: 'He closed his robe and walked to the window, again gazing out at the mystical city before him'.

This mystical city is a suitable setting for a cosmic drama, a great contest between the forces of good and evil that is played out in the actions of the characters, the allusions, the symbols, and in many other layers of reference in *The Lost Symbol*.

THE ANCIENT MYSTERIES

Robert Langdon and Mal'akh are each determined, for their very different reasons, to discover the key to the Ancient Mysteries. But what do the Ancient Mysteries amount to? 'The entire essence of the Ancient Mysteries', says Katherine Solomon, 'is hovering over the Rotunda'. She is referring to *The Apotheosis of Washington* at the apex of the dome of the Capitol Building, a fresco that Langdon sees as 'the great promise of man becoming God' (chapter 133). The idea that man is or should seek to become divine is not supported by mainstream Christianity but belongs to Gnostic heresies or to pre-Christian belief, to the world of the Greeks and Romans and the ancient Egyptians. It is also a tenet of Mormonism, which in part grew out of Freemasonry, and is found in various Eastern belief systems flourishing today. If the Bible were properly interpreted, says Dan Brown, it would likewise be understood to proclaim the divinity of man, but it needs to be read in the light of what he calls 'the lost wisdom of all the ages'.

One of Dan Brown's sources for that lost wisdom is acknowledged in the epigraph preceding *The Lost Symbol*: 'To live in the world without becoming aware of the meaning of the world is like wandering about in a great library without touching the books.' The source of the quotation is given as *The Secret Teachings of All Ages*, but for some reason Dan Brown chose not to give the name of its author (though he mentions him by name in chapter 133). He is Manly Palmer Hall, a Canadian-born mystic – 'philosopher', Brown calls him – who spent most of his life in Los Angeles and died there in 1990. *The Secret Teachings of All Ages*, published in 1928 when Hall was twenty-seven, immediately established his reputation in esoteric circles. Its forty-eight chapters bear such headings as 'The Ancient Mysteries and Secret Societies', 'The Initiation of the Pyramid', 'Freemasonic Symbolism' and 'Mystic Christianity'. Hall was him-

Peter Solomon's hand points towards the fresco in the dome of the Capitol Rotunda, Constantino Brumidi's *The Apotheosis of Washington*. A marble statue of George Washington is in the foreground.

self a Freemason and was initiated into the Thirty-third Degree by the Supreme Council of the Scottish Rite in 1973.

The Secret Teachings is a useful resource for those wanting to delve deeper into the notions found in *The Lost Symbol*, and Hall's writings will be examined later in this book, together with *The Book of the Dead*, *The Key of Solomon*, various works of the Hermetica, Gnosticism and the Kabbalah, as well as accounts of the Mystery Religions and the philosophies of the Graeco-Roman and Egyptian worlds – the sum sources of the Ancient Mysteries.

ADEPTS THROUGH THE AGES

The Ancient Mysteries are with us, but you have to know where to look, and more importantly how to look. The secrets of the Ancient Mysteries are encoded in the writings of Pythagoras, Hermes, Heraclitus and Paracelsus, we are told by *The Lost Symbol* in chapter 129, and they were also hidden in the ancient Library of Alexandria before it was destroyed. 'The enlightened Adepts who possessed this knowledge vowed to keep it veiled from the masses because it was considered far too potent and dangerous for the uninitiated' (chapter 19). Among the adepts were Buddha, Jesus, Mohammed and Zoroaster (chapter 130), and their sacred works are encoded too. As Peter Solomon says to Langdon (chapter 131), 'There is a *reason* Christian monks spend lifetimes attempting to decipher the Bible. There is a *reason* that Jewish mystics and Kabbalists pore over the Old Testament. And that *reason*, Robert, is that there exist powerful secrets hidden in the pages of this ancient book … a vast collection of untapped wisdom waiting to be unveiled.'

Thanks to the efforts of a succession of adepts, the Ancient Mysteries have been saved and transmitted, still in codified form, to modern times. Dan Brown identifies the German Renaissance artist Albrecht Dürer as 'a lifelong student of the Ancient Mysteries. To this day, nobody fully understands the messages hidden in Dürer's art' (chapter 68). Dürer's famous engraving *Melencolia I*, which hangs in Washington's National Gallery of Art, 'depicts mankind's struggle to comprehend the Ancient Mysteries'. As it happens, this engraving serves Robert Langdon well, for it reveals a Magic Square that proves to be a vital clue in decrypting the message encoded in the Masonic Pyramid that Solomon had entrusted to his symbologist friend for safekeeping. What else *Melencolia I* reveals, or hides, will be discussed later in this book.

Another great figure in the line of transmission of the Ancient Mysteries, says Dan Brown, was the English scientist Sir Isaac Newton, 'whose name had always been a recurring guidepost for those seeking secret knowledge' (chapter 85). Newton was the author of the *Principia Mathematica*, published in 1687, which described gravitation and the laws of motion, a work that was central to the scientific revolution and the acceptance that rational investigation can reveal the inner workings of nature. Yet Newton was convinced that this was merely a rediscovery of ancient knowledge. In a 1942 lecture to the Royal Society, of which Newton was an early president, John Maynard Keynes said that Newton was 'not the first of the age of reason. He was the last of the magicians'. He was more than that, according to *The Lost Symbol*: 'Like the ancient Adepts, he understood himself as divine' (chapter 85). Certainly Newton rejected the Trinity and the divinity of Jesus, putting himself in that long line of heresies that has included Arians, Gnostics and Cathars.

The way Dan Brown tells it, after the suppression of the mystery schools of Egypt, the Ancient Mysteries went underground but surfaced again in seventeenth-century London. The Royal Society, founded in 1660 and the oldest scientific institution in the world, grew out of a loose network of scientists and intellectuals who called themselves 'the Invisible College' (chapter 30). Dan Brown wrongly describes the Society as a 'concealed college', enigmatic and elite, and he is wrong in listing Sir Francis Bacon among the members of the Society or its precursor. But Bacon did encourage the Society's creation through his book *New Atlantis* with its tale of 'an Order or Society which we call "Salomon's House"', an institute for 'the finding out of the true nature of all things'. You might also see in Salomon's House an inspiration for the Smithsonian Institute of which Peter Solomon is director in *The Lost Symbol*. In the modern day, as Brown correctly observes, members of the Royal Society have included Albert Einstein and Stephen Hawking; he also cites that remarkable polymath and Founding Father of the United States, Benjamin Franklin, who lived abroad in France and England for over twenty years and was also a Freemason.

THE FREEMASONS

According to Robert Langdon in chapter 30 of *The Lost Symbol*, the Freemasons are the last surviving custodians of the Ancient Mysteries. Previously there had been a number of secret brotherhoods who had protected the Mysteries; they took care to share their knowledge with fellow adepts, and passed their wisdom from generation to generation only through properly trained initiates. These secret societies had been formed against the threat that the Mysteries might fall into the wrong hands with devastating effect, but by the sixteenth century, almost all of these very same European societies had been destroyed by successive waves of religious persecution, until only the Freemasons remained. Langdon goes on to explain how the Ancient Mysteries came to America. Fearing that their own brotherhood might die off one day, and that the Ancient Mysteries would be lost for all time, the Freemasons transported their secret wisdom from the Old World to the New – to America, a land they hoped would remain free of religious tyranny.

The very heart of Freemasonry in America, says *The Lost Symbol*, is one and the same with the national capital of the United States.

In 1793 George Washington himself, dressed in his Freemason's apron and performing the full Masonic ritual, laid the cornerstone of the Capitol Building. 'This city had been conceived and designed

George Washington in Masonic attire, holding a trowel.

by Master Masons – George Washington, Ben Franklin, and Pierre L'Enfant – powerful minds who adorned their new capital with Masonic symbolism, architecture, and art.' There was nothing simply decorative or ceremonial about these proceedings. 'Washington, DC', says Langdon, 'has more astrological signs in its architecture than any other city in the world – zodiacs, star charts, cornerstones laid at precise astrological dates and times. More than half of the framers of our Constitution were Masons, men who strongly believed that the stars and fate were intertwined, men who paid close attention to the layout of the heavens as they structured their new world' (chapter 6). This belief in the correspondance between the heavens and the earth echoes the words ascribed to Hermes Trismegistus, 'As above, so below'; it is the essence of Hermetism, of the Ancient Mysteries. More to the point, it expresses a belief in a correspondance between the macrocosm (the universe) and the microcosm (ourselves), and is the basis for the argument that each man is God.

THE RELIGIOUS BELIEFS OF THE FOUNDING FATHERS

As part of his argument that the Bible has been distorted and mis-understood, Dan Brown introduces as witnesses no less a group of figures than the Founding Fathers of the United States. John Adams, Benjamin Franklin and Thomas Paine 'all warned of the profound dangers of interpreting the Bible literally. In fact, Thomas Jefferson was so convinced the Bible's true message was hidden that he literally cut up the pages and reedited the book, attempting, in his words, "to do away with the artificial scaffolding and restore the genuine doctrines"' (chapter 131).

Given that the present-day United States is the most religious country in the industrialized world, this would be remarkable if true. And yet the chaplain of the Continental Congress and a close observer of George Washington stated unequivocally, 'I do not believe that any degree of recollection will bring to my mind any fact which would prove General Washington to have been a believer in the Christian revelation'.

So what was the religious position of America's Founding Fathers, and what concept of God, if any, did they have in mind when they established the United States? Some, like Washington, were Freemasons; did they also believe that man was God? Later chapters will examine their beliefs and the spiritual values that attended the birth of the revolutionary republic.

TRANSFORMATIONS

Several of the best scenes in *The Lost Symbol* are to do with transformation, such as when Mal'akh seals Robert Langdon in a box and pumps it full of liquid. 'All he could do now was stare up through the blur of water above him and hope.' Unable to hold his breath any longer, 'His lips parted. His lungs expanded. And the liquid came pouring in. ... And then blackness. Robert Langdon was gone' (chapter 103). But not quite, it turns out, for this scene corresponds to the tenth hour of the Amduat, that part of the Egyptian Book of the Dead which deals with the soul's passage through the twelve hours of the night, when bodies of the deceased are suspended in the primeval waters of Nun. They appear to be drowning, but in fact they are being refreshed by the waters, and the promise is that they will be resurrected. 'O ye whose cheeks are filled with water, whose souls have been deprived of their heavenly air, and who beat the air with your hands in order to obtain it, Come ye forth in this stream, for your members shall not perish, and your flesh shall not decay, and ye shall have dominion over the water, and your souls will have life.' It is not a spell that saves Langdon from drowning, rather science, for in fact he has been submerged in an oxygen-rich perfluorocarbon liquid – not something invented by Dan Brown,

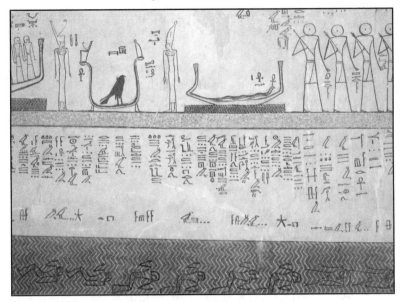

'...Ye shall have dominion over the water, and your souls will have life' – Langdon's aquatic ordeal corresponds to the tenth hour of the Amduat from the *Egyptian Book of the Dead.*

but a substance that is already finding medical uses.

As Langdon is undergoing his passage through the waters of Nun, Katherine is nearby, strapped to a chair, being drained of her blood by a medical needle stuck into her arm. 'A human hour glass', says Mal'akh (chapter 107) as he leaves her to die. Mal'akh is performing a ritual on Katherine that he has already performed on countless small animals. He began his career of demonic evil when one night a crow flew in through his open window and was unable to escape. Clutching the bird in one hand, and placing it over a makeshift altar, Mal'akh pierced the large vein in its right wing while repeating an incantation: 'Camiach, Eomiahe, Emial, Macbal, Emoii, Zazean ... by the most holy names of the angels in the Book of Assamaian, I conjure thee that thou assist me in this operation by the power of the One True God'.

Just as Dan Brown does not himself mention the Amduat, neither does he say that Mal'akh is taking a leaf straight out of *The Key of Solomon*, a medieval book of magic containing exactly that ritual and incantation. Amid the most outrageous of his scenes, Brown is enjoying a few private moments of authenticity.

The theme of transformation runs throughout *The Lost Symbol*. Mal'akh adorns himself with tattoos. 'The act of tattooing one's skin was a transformative declaration of power, an announcement to the world: *I am in control of my own flesh. … The human spirit craves mastery over its carnal shell*' (chapter 2). For Mal'akh it is part of a perverted attempt to become a god, which culminates with the scene when he offers himself as a blood sacrifice in the upper chamber

The House of the Temple – with a pinnacle the shape of a stepped Mesoamerican pyramid.

of the House of the Temple, the headquarters of the Scottish Rite Freemasons, Southern Jurisdiction. Its pinnacle is built in the shape of a stepped pyramid, like the Mesoamerican pyramids where the living hearts of human beings were cut out from their breasts and offered to the gods.

But the greatest transformation envisioned in *The Lost Symbol* is found in Katherine Solomon's work in noetic science, which reaches towards the discovery of a universal consciousness and the godlike ability for thought to control the world around it; and in the corresponding conviction of her brother Peter Solomon that we are on the verge of the apotheosis of man, the transformation of the human mind into its true potentiality.

The Epilogue brings Robert's transformational twelve-hour journey to a close. 'Langdon thought about all he had learned tonight. He thought of Katherine's belief that everything was about to change. He thought of Peter's faith that an age of enlightenment was imminent. And he thought of the words of a great prophet who had boldly declared: *Nothing is hidden that will not be made known; nothing is secret that will not come to light.*' That prophet is Jesus, and the lines are repeated twice in the Bible, at Luke 8:17 and Luke 12:2.

The reality behind the science, the technology, the philosophy and the spiritual quest for transformation as set out in *The Lost Symbol* is as fascinating and puzzling as the symbols Langdon must decode. It is critically examined in the further pages of this book.

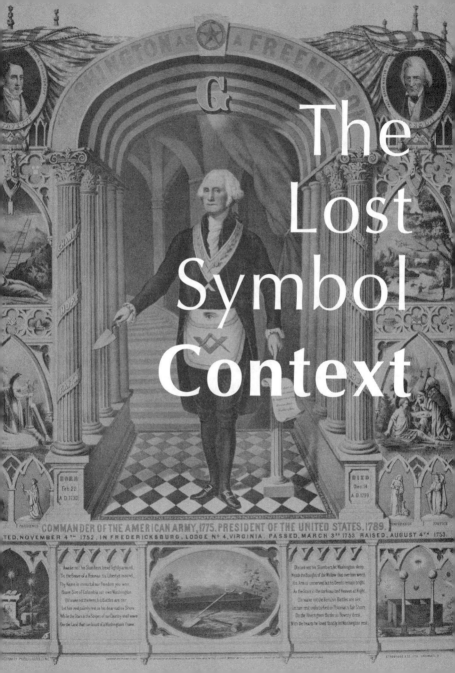

The Lost Symbol Context

COMMANDER OF THE AMERICAN ARMY, 1775, PRESIDENT OF THE UNITED STATES, 1789,

TED, NOVEMBER 4 TH 1752, IN FREDERICKSBURG, LODGE N° 4, VIRGINIA, PASSED, MARCH 3 RD 1753 RAISED, AUGUST 4 TH 1753.

The
Characters

WHAT'S IN A NAME?

'"My name is Dr Christopher Abaddon. I was hoping I might talk to you for a moment about your brother?" ... Katherine did not recognize the name.'

THE LOST SYMBOL [CHAPTER 22]

Katherine Solomon could have saved herself a lot of trouble had she recognized the meaning of Dr Christopher Abaddon's surname. Abaddon appears in the Bible's Book of Revelation 9:11 as the angel of the bottomless pit; his name means 'the destroyer'. Dr Abaddon is Mal'akh in disguise. He was born as Zachary Solomon, the son of Peter Solomon; for a time he called himself Andros Dareios before he finally transformed himself into the monstrous Mal'akh. The names Dan Brown gives his characters can be clues to the story, and they can enrich its meaning.

MAL'AKH THE WOULD-BE GOD

Zachary Solomon, alias Andros Dareios, the future Mal'akh, discovered his destiny in John Milton's *Paradise Lost*: 'He read of the great fallen angel ... the warrior demon who fought against the light ... the valiant one ... the angel called Moloch. *Moloch walked the earth as a god*. The angel's name, Andros later learned, when translated

The pagan god Moloch as visualized by the American artist John Singer Sargent in his ambitious mural cycle *The Triumph of Religion* at Boston Public Library. The murals were completed over a span of thirty years from 1890 to 1919.

to the ancient tongue, became Mal'akh' (chapter 77). In Milton's poem, Moloch is worshipped as a god who demands the sacrifice of children; and as he makes his appearance in *Paradise Lost* at the head of a host of demons, we are reminded that he has deceived Solomon into defiling Jerusalem's holiest spot by building a temple to Moloch and outraging God himself.

> First, Moloch, horrid king besmeared with blood
> Of human sacrifice, and parents' tears.
> ... The wisest heart
> Of Solomon he led by fraud to build
> His temple right against the temple of God

Paradise Lost, Book 1, lines 392ff

Mal'akh will likewise deceive his own father, Peter Solomon, who in the Prologue to *The Lost Symbol* initiates him, without realizing who he is, into the Thirty-third Degree. The secrets of the ceremony and the identities of the people at the ceremony are secretly filmed by Mal'akh as part of his plan to destroy Freemasonry and indeed to bring down the American government and cause a catastrophic international crisis.

Some Real People Behind the Characters

Sometimes the names of Dan Brown's characters are anagrams of real people. Jonas Faukman, Robert Langdon's editor in chapter 44, is an anagram of Dan Brown's editor Jason Kaufman who appears in the acknowledgements at the front of *The Lost Symbol*. Nola Kaye, the fictional analyst in the CIA's Security Office, is a partial anagram for a woman famous in cryptographical circles as Elonka. Her full name is Elonka Dunin, and she is generally considered the world's foremost expert on the Kryptos sculpture (see p.205) which stands within the grounds of the CIA's headquarters at Langley, Virginia, and which makes an appearance in chapter 127 of Dan Brown's book.

Trish Dunne, Katherine Solomon's assistant, is also a tribute, in this case to Brenda Dunne, manager of the Princeton Engineering Anomalies Research laboratory, or PEAR (see p.158), that conducted studies in extrasensory perception and telekinesis which contributed towards work elsewhere in noetics. At least two women see Katherine Solomon as a nod to themselves: the blonde Marilyn Schlitz, President of the Institute of Noetic Sciences (see p.161), and Lynne McTaggart (see p.163), author of *The Intention Experiment*, a book mentioned in *The Lost Symbol*, who pointedly remarks that, unlike Marilyn Schlitz, she has black hair like Katherine.

ROBERT LANGDON

The invention of the name Robert Langdon was straightforward; it is Dan Brown's tribute to his friend John Langdon, a Professor of Typography at Drexel University in Philadelphia who created a series of ambigrams – words that can be read both right side up and upside down – for the first Robert Langdon novel, *Angels and Demons*. But leaving aside Dan Brown's tribute to his friend, who really is Robert Langdon? As it happens, both Brown and Langdon were born in Exeter, New Hampshire, on 22 June; Brown in 1964, Langdon in 1956. Both attended Phillips Exeter Academy, one of the top private schools in the United States. And both have a fondness for wearing turtleneck shirts, Harris Tweed jackets, khaki trousers and slip-on shoes. In the public mind Robert Langdon has now become identified with Tom Hanks, the actor who has played the role in the film versions of *Angels and Demons* and *The Da Vinci Code*, but Dan Brown does not see it that way. 'I spent a few months on a movie set. But I've spent years in my head with this other character I've created.' So does Dan Brown see himself in Robert Langdon? Not exactly, but he does admit that 'Langdon's the guy I wish I could be.'

SOLOMON THE WISE

The 58-year-old Peter Solomon is Robert Langdon's friend and mentor. Their relationship goes back thirty years. According to Langdon, he is the one man, apart from his late father, that 'I never want to disappoint'. Solomon is introduced in *The Lost Symbol* as a mild-mannered academic who is nevertheless the scion of a powerful and remarkable family, founders and patrons of institutions all across the nation: 'Like the Rothschilds in Europe, the surname Solomon had always carried the mystique of American royalty and success' (chapter 3). The name Solomon and the suggestion of royalty immediately bring to mind the great King Solomon of the Old Testament, famous for his power and wisdom and for building the fabled Temple of Solomon in Jerusalem nearly three thousand years ago.

There is a scene in *The Lost Symbol*, chapter 61, in which Peter Solomon offers his son Zachary a choice. The boy has turned eighteen and has come of age to inherit his share of the family fortune. The money is his now if he insists, but Solomon would first like him to complete his education within the Freemasons, for that would give him wisdom, and he would also then be given the Masonic Pyramid which is the key to the Ancient Mysteries, the key to great human transformation. 'You will emerge with the maturity to receive both your money *and* this pyramid. Wealth and wisdom. A potent combination.' But Zachary wants the money now and rejects wisdom, a choice that leads to the calamities and evils that follow.

Here *The Lost Symbol* is inviting a comparison with the opposite choice made by King Solomon. When Solomon, whose name means peace, was raised to the throne of Israel and Judah, he was asked by God what he desired, and Solomon answered: 'Give thy servant an understanding heart to judge thy people, that I may discern between good and bad.' God was pleased that Solomon had asked for understanding and not for riches or a long life, and he

King Solomon has often been depicted as a powerful monarch and judge but French artist Gustave Doré's Solomon, from his illustrated English Bible, cuts a more vulnerable figure here, more in common with Brown's character who spends most of the novel injured in a wheelchair.

replied, 'Lo, I have given thee a wise and an understanding heart; so that there was none like thee before thee, neither after thee shall any arise like unto thee. And I have also given thee that which thou has not asked, both riches and honour: so that there shall not be any among the kings like unto thee all thy days' (1 Kings 3:5–14). Indeed, according to the Bible Solomon's reign was marked by prosperity and prestige, his wisdom was said to excel even all the wisdom of Egypt (1 Kings 4:30), and he has come down to us as the wise man par excellence.

But Solomon has also excited the popular imagination as a builder, a mystic, a magician and a utopian seer. Suggestions of these various aspects come into play in *The Lost Symbol*, as will be seen in the sections below on the Freemasons, the Ancient Mysteries and the Adepts.

WHAT IS FREEMASONRY?

A good way to answer that question is to ask the Freemasons in Dan Brown's home town of Exeter, New Hampshire. Star in the East Lodge No.59 is at 63 Water Street and is part of the 1st Masonic District of Free and Accepted Masons under the Grand Lodge of Free and Accepted Masons of the State of New Hampshire. It was constituted on 23 April 1857. Our thanks to Stephen Murad for setting out the tenets and principles of Freemasonry.

Freemasonry is a system of morality and ethics that transcends political, racial, financial and secular boundaries. It is a belief that all men are created equal, and all deserve respect, love, relief and charity. It is a voluntary association of men who have adopted its teachings as a way of life, and seek to improve themselves in their daily existence. It is a pursuit of excellence in a world where excellence seems unattainable. Teaching morality through symbolism and allegory, its rites and ceremonies instruct its members to cherish the tenets of the 'Brotherhood of Man, under the Fatherhood of God'.

It is sometimes easier to tell non-Masons what Freemasonry is not. It is not an organization that solicits membership – all men must come to Freemasonry of their own free will and accord. It is not an insurance organization or a benefit society. It is not a religion, a creed, or a religious order. It is not a charity, but recognizes that the tenet of Charity as a foundation of love for humanity is a duty for all Masons. It is not organized for profit, and no member may profit from his association with the Fraternity, upon penalty of expulsion. It does not dictate to any man as to his religious or secular beliefs and is not a substitute for the connection any man has to his God. It is never a forum for discussion of religion, politics, or other partisan affairs. Finally, it is not a secret society as it does not conceal its existence, or its purpose.

Freemasonry seeks to improve all men who would believe that there is a fundamental good in everyone who is not unwilling to live to its precepts.

The Freemasons

THE OLDEST SURVIVING SECRET SOCIETY IN THE WORLD?

'They are fascinating because we live in a world where different cultures are killing each other over whose version of God is accurate. And here you have a global organization that is spiritual and yet will bring Muslims, Jews, Christians and even just people who are confused about religion – bring them together and say we all agree that there is some good big thing out there but we're not going to put a label on it; let's worship together. The mystery is in their origins and in the fact that they have managed to remain pretty secret. Their rituals are arcane.'

DAN BROWN, TELEVISION INTERVIEW, 15 SEPTEMBER 2009

The version of Freemasonry Dan Brown refers to in *The Lost Symbol* is the Scottish Rite, which has nothing to do with Scotland nor with global Masonry, and exists almost exclusively in the United States, where it was invented in the nineteenth century. To the three degrees of Freemasonry as established in Britain and recognized around the world, the Scottish Rite has added what are sometimes called 'higher degrees', right up to the Thirty-third Degree. But 'higher' is the wrong word; they are really side dishes, so to speak. It is as though you had studied to become a master chef (the three degrees of Freemasonry); you might then want to busy yourself making an apple pie, a cherry pie, a gooseberry pie, etc (the Scottish Rite); you have not moved beyond being a master chef, but you have made a lot of pies. The Scottish Rite is not much found outside the United States and it is not recognized in Britain where Freemasonry began. It is important to know the history and significance of Freemasonry itself before looking at the Scottish Rite.

ORIGINS OF FREEMASONRY

At a time when most workers were tied to the land, masons were freelancers who sought work where they could, and in Scotland and England during the Middle Ages they began to form themselves into mutual help associations. There were two kinds of masons, the 'rough masons' who worked in hard stone, laying foundations and raising walls, and the more mobile masons who carved the fine façades on cathedrals from softer stone. This softer stone was known as freestone, and the elite masons who worked with it were called freestone masons, or freemasons for short. As the freemasons travelled around Britain they would stay at lodges, and after the Reformation in the sixteenth century one of their activities at their lodges was reading the Bible. The Catholic Church had discouraged the translation of the Bible into the vernacular, fearing that the Bible would replace the Papacy as the font of authority. This was precisely what Protestants in Scotland and England were eager to see happen, for the Bible was discovered to have revolutionary implications; for example, it spoke of prophets who had overthrown wicked kings, and at the same time it failed to support the notion that the bishop of Rome, that is the Pope, should be the supreme leader of a universal Church.

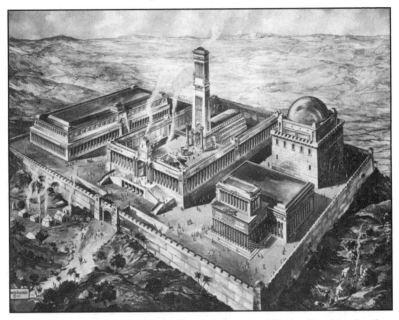

An artist's impression of King Solomon's temple from 1913 based on the reconstruction work of biblical archaeologist John Wesley Kelchner.

On the other hand, Protestants decided that the Bible was itself the word of God, and those who were freemasons paid close attention to the Second Book of Chronicles, with its description of how Solomon asked Hiram, the king of Tyre, to build the Temple in Jersualem. They paid particular attention to the detailed measurements of the Temple, which God would only have troubled to mention, in their view, because they contained some profound theological truths. The freemasons were especially impressed by that other Hiram, not Hiram the king of Tyre, but Hiram the widow's son, the one they chose to call Hiram Abiff. The most remarkable work at Solomon's Temple had been done by Hiram Abiff: the casting of the enormous basin known as the Sea of Bronze and of the huge bronze pillars known as Jachin and Boaz. As the Bible said, this Hiram was a man 'filled with wisdom and understanding'.

The efficacy of these freemasons' mutual assistance associations depended on their exclusivity, on their being clubs open to freemasons only, and the point was made by developing a system of signs and rituals supposedly passed down from ancient times and by means of which adherents gained access to private meetings. One such ritual concerned Hiram Abiff, to whom the masons gave a history that went far beyond his brief mention in the Bible. Hiram Abiff, they said, knew the secret of the Temple. Three villains kidnapped Hiram and threatened to kill him if he did not reveal the secret 'Master's word' – a term used by the masons in their trade to differentiate the pay and assignments of workers, but also, as the ritual now implied, bearing deeper and mystical significance. But Hiram refused to reveal the secret, and his assailants murdered him.

When Solomon heard about this, he wondered what Hiram's secret was, and he sent three masons to look for his body, also telling them that if they could not find the secret, then the first thing they saw when they found Hiram's body should itself become the secret of the Temple. The masons found Hiram Abiff's coffin, and when they opened it the first thing they saw was his hand – and from this the masons made the handshake and other signs of recognition the new secret. On the basis of this story, the masons developed the ritual by which a Freemason advances through three degrees, from Apprentice Mason to Entered Apprentice, and so to the Third Degree, Master Mason. Advancing to the Third Degree requires that the initiate must agree to undergo the sufferings of Hiram Abiff should he ever reveal the Freemasons' secrets, and that if he ever breaks his oath it would be right for his fellow Freemasons to cut out his heart, his liver and his entrails, in the same way as a traitor was disembowelled as part of the process of being hanged, drawn and quartered.

THE FOUNDING OF THE GRAND LODGE: WHAT TO DO ABOUT GOD

But already these associations of artisan freemasons were undergoing a transition that would alter their fundamental nature. To enhance the standing of their associations, and perhaps to deflect criticism that they were subversive organizations, freemasons invited influential people to serve as patrons. This gave the freemasons a social appeal which together with their study of the Bible began to attract an enquiring elite comprising gentlemen and scholars, professionals and merchants, so that by about 1700 these 'admitted' or 'speculative masons' outnumbered 'operative masons', as the artisans were called. In fact, the modern institution that we recognize as Freemasonry was born when a group of four London lodges made up of both operative and admitted masons merged in 1717 to create a Grand Lodge. They placed at their head not a practising mason but a gentleman, and never again would a true stonemason serve as a Grand Master.

A further important change came when James Anderson, a Scottish-born Presbyterian minister and the master of a London lodge, was commissioned to write a constitution for the Grand Lodge of England to standardize the practices and rituals of lodges operating under its aegis. In his *Constitutions*, published in 1723, he shifted the Freemasons away from their exclusively Christian conception of God towards the more generalized concept of a Great Architect of the Universe. 'A Mason is obliged by his Tenure, to obey the moral law; and if he rightly understands the Art, he will never be a stupid Atheist nor an irreligious Libertine. But though in ancient times Masons were charged in every country to be of the religion of that country or nation, whatever it was, yet it is now thought more expedient only to oblige them to that religion in which all men agree, leaving their particular Opinions to themselves: that is, to be Good men and

James Anderson's *Constitutions* (1723) was commissioned to standardize Masonic rituals and practice.

True, or Men of Honour and Honesty, by whatever Denomination or Persuasion they may be distinguished; whereby Masonry becomes the Centre of Union and the Means of conciliating true Friendship among persons that must have remained at a perpetual distance.'

Anderson swept away doctrinal distinctions in favour of a common denominator that all could agree with in the form of the Great Architect of the Universe, meaning that all denominations were invited to join, and not only Christians, for soon Jews were joining the Freemasons too. His reform also made allowance for Deism, a way of conceiving God that had developed in England during the latter part of the seventeenth century and was now established among many thinking people in Britain, France and Germany, and had spread to America too. Deists accepted only those beliefs that were rationally warranted; faith was not enough. For some, this meant that God was the creator but took no interest in the world. He did not intervene in nature nor in human affairs. He neither revealed himself to man nor responded to prayer, nor was there an afterlife. The Bible was not the word of God, and Jesus was not the Son of God. Other deists, while rejecting revelation and miracles, gave themselves to prayer and held open the possibility of an afterlife. Deists were not atheists; the universe was proof of God's existence. But they were far from being orthodox Christians, if they counted themselves Christians at all. Not all Freemasons were Deists, but certainly some were.

Though Anderson's *Constitutions* was imbued with contemporary Protestant ideals of morality, merit and political equality, these overlapped with Enlightenment values of freedom, democracy and reason, which had the effect of breaking through religious dogmas that had circumscribed thought. It was also a celebration of geometry and architecture as practised from ancient times, accompanied by detailed descriptions of the Seven Wonders of the Ancient World, which were given as the Great Pyramid, Solomon's Temple, the City and Hanging Gardens of Babylon, the Tomb of Mausolus, the Pharos at Alexandria, Phidias's statue of Jupiter at Olympia and the Colossus at Rhodes.

Yet at the same time the *Constitutions* was accompanied by a fanciful history of the Freemasons from Adam to the reign of George I based on an exegesis of the Old Testament – for example, 'The Israelites, at their leaving Egypt, were a whole Kingdom of Masons, under the Conduct of their Grand Master Moses'. And then there was the familiar Hiram Abiff: 'After the Erection of Solomon's Temple, Masonry was improv'd in all the neighbouring Nations; for the many Artists employed about it, under Hiram Abif, after it was finish'd, dispers'd themselves into Syria, Mesopotamia, Assyria,

Chaldea, Babylonia, Media, Persia, Arabia, Africa, Lesser Asia, Greece and other Parts of Europe, where they taught this liberal Art to the free born Sons of eminent Persons, by whose Dexterity the Kings, Princes, and Potentates, built many glorious Piles, and became the Grand Masters, each in his own Territory.' For all that educated people of the Enlightenment looked towards the future, they also looked back towards the past, for they believed that antiquity had possessed much learning and wisdom that had since been lost, and that it was their duty to recover what they could from Biblical and classical times.

This 1723 edition of the *Constitutions* was edited and reprinted by Benjamin Franklin in Philadelphia in 1734; it was the first Masonic book printed in America.

MYSTERY AND ROMANCE: INVENTING THE SCOTTISH RITE

News of the formation of London's Grand Lodge and the activities of British Freemasons soon spread across Europe. By the 1730s masonic lodges had been founded in the Netherlands, France, Germany and elsewhere in Europe, often by representatives of the London Grand Lodge who travelled abroad for the purpose, but sometimes by local residents who were inspired by the Grand Lodge but were not under its direction. One reason that Freemasonry proved popular in Europe was that it was imported from Britain, home of the Glorious Revolution of 1688 that had definitively curtailed the powers of the king and divided authority between the monarchy, Parliament and the judiciary, and that had instituted a degree of religious toleration. Britain was widely admired by the people of Europe as a progressive and tolerant nation, even if its institutions and inventions, not least Freemasonry, were deeply distrusted by Europe's autocratic rulers and the Catholic Church.

For all that the Freemasons of Britain possessed a cult of secrecy and linked this to a mysterious knowledge associated with Solomon's Temple, they were nevertheless a sensible and innocuous fraternal organization whose lodges fulfilled a similar function to that of the London coffee houses or social clubs. But it seems that before Freemasonry could take root on the continent of Europe, it needed to be imbued with several extra doses of exotic colouring and occult myth.

The first step was taken in 1736 or 1737 by a Scotsman called Andrew Michael Ramsay, a Jacobite exile living in France who, as chancellor of the French Grand Lodge, introduced a fictitious Crusader background to the Freemasons and notions of aristocratic class. British Freemasonry was democratic in nature; its members included artisans and aristocrats, professional men, learned men and middle-class traders, all content to rub shoulders with one another. But neither rubbing shoulders nor belonging to an institution that had grown from working-men's beginnings appealed to the upper strata of French society. The gentry and nobility of France wanted recognition of social distinctions, and they wanted it reinforced by style, nostalgia and romance. Ramsay gave it to them by the bucketful, suggesting that the stonemasons had also been knightly warriors in the Holy Land, and soon he had turned the French Freemasons into an ancient chivalrous international secret society. 'Our ancestors, the Crusaders, who had come from all parts of Christendom to the Holy Land, wanted to group persons from every nation in a single spiritual confraternity', Ramsay announced in his Oration to Saint John's Lodge in Paris, variously dated 27 December 1736 or 21 March 1737.

In Ramsay's version of the past, the Crusaders had attempted to restore the Temple of Solomon in a hostile environment and had devised a system of secret signs and rituals to protect themselves against their Muslim enemy, who otherwise would infiltrate their positions and cut their throats. Ramsay also said that after the collapse of the Crusader states in the Middle East, the knights returned to their homelands in Europe and established Freemason lodges there. But their lodges and their rites were neglected over time and it was only among Scotsmen that the Freemasons preserved their former splendour: 'Since that time Great Britain became the seat of our Order, the conservator of our laws and the depository of our secrets ... From the British Isles the Royal Art is now repassing into France ... In this happy age when love of peace has become the virtue of heroes, this nation, one of the most spiritual in Europe, will become the centre of the Order. She will clothe our work, our statutes, our customs with grace, delicacy and good taste, essential qualities of the Order, of which the basis is wisdom, strength and beauty of genius. It is in future in our Lodges, as it were in public schools, that Frenchmen shall learn, without travelling, the characters of all nations and that strangers shall experience that France is the home of all nations.'

Ramsay said nothing about the Knights Templar, that order of fighting knights founded in Jerusalem in 1119 to defend pilgrims visiting the Holy Land. Perhaps he was wary of offending the still powerful French monarchy and Church – it was after all Philip IV, ancestor of the dynasty of kings still ruling France, who, together with an Inquisition composed of docile French bishops, had destroyed the Templars four centuries earlier, burning Jacques de Molay, their last Grand Master, at the stake in 1314. Instead, Ramsay referred to the Knights of St John of Jerusalem, the Hospitallers, who still existed in Malta in his day. But it was not long before the lively French Masonic mind altered the identity of Ramsay's order, substituting for the Hospitallers the dramatic and mysterious – and conveniently extinct – order of the Templars. The fancy soon took wing.

The Ecossaise or Scottish Degrees, as the French called the profusion of mystic and chivalric degrees that were generated after

Andrew Michael Ramsay's romanticized Freemasonry was introduced to France, eventually found their way to America. In 1763 Estienne Morin, who had been appointed Grand Inspector to all parts of the New World by the Ecossaise lodge in Bordeaux, established a 25-degree Rite of Perfection in Haiti, which at that time was the French colony of Saint-Domingue. From there it spread to French colonial New Orleans in 1764, to New York in 1767 and then after the success of the War of Independence to Charleston, South Carolina, in 1783. Charleston proved to be the birthplace of the Scottish Rite of 33 degrees, but not until 1801, after which it spread rapidly through the South but took another 67 years to become well established in the North. After the American Civil War the Scottish Rite became a national institution, though one that nevertheless, then as now, could not exist independently of the three degrees, which can only be conferred at a Craft Lodge or Blue Lodge like those originally warranted by one of the Grand Lodges (see box opposite). But before looking at the great flowering of the Scottish Rite under Albert Pike in the late-nineteenth-century United States, we need to explore the peculiar history of Freemasonry in colonial and revolutionary America.

THE STRANGE STORY OF BENJAMIN FRANKLIN

In 1724 the eighteen-year-old Benjamin Franklin went to London, where he hoped to meet the aged Isaac Newton. He never managed to do so, but he did meet Freemasons, and brought back with him to America Anderson's *Constitutions*, which had been published the year before. In 1731 he joined a newly opened lodge in Philadelphia, the earliest lodge in America for which there is documentary proof, and by 1734, the year in which he published the American edition of the *Constitutions*, he had been raised to the Third Degree and became master of his lodge. Eventually Franklin became head of the order in Pennsylvania.

DEGREES AND 'HIGHER' DEGREES: FREEMASONS AND THE SCOTTISH RITE

The three degrees of Freemasonry – Apprentice Mason, Entered Apprentice and finally Master Mason – are 'worked' (that is obtained) at the local lodge, called a Craft Lodge in Britain, a Blue Lodge in America (nobody knows what 'Blue' means nor where the name came from); the rituals are based on the story of Hiram Abiff and Solomon's Temple. The third degree of Master Mason is the top degree in Freemasonry worldwide; there is no higher degree.

But when Freemasonry travelled from Britain to France in the eighteenth century, fanciful new titles and rituals were devised. As we have seen, these were not recognized by the original Grand Lodge in London, but they did find their way to America, where in 1801 they were organized into a system of appendant degrees called the Scottish Rite. These are truly appendages, for they are stuck on to the first three degrees of Freemasonry; nobody can join the Scottish Rite without first becoming a Master Mason, and that can only be achieved at a local Craft or Blue Lodge. The Scottish Rite cannot create Freemasons; and no matter how many degrees you pass through in the Scottish Rite you are never higher than a master mason.

In the United States, each of the 'higher' degrees, from four to thirty-two, is presented in an auditorium to gatherings of candidates who may number in the dozens, hundreds, even thousands at a time, which partly explains the existence of huge Scottish Rite cathedrals which look as though they have come straight out of the Middle Ages. Passing through each degree amounts to watching a one-act dramatic play performed by a cast backed by a technical crew and complete with sets, costumes, lighting, sound effects and so on.

Just as theatre was used in Greek and Roman times, and right through the Middle Ages, to examine ideas and to instruct, so Freemasons use it to present ancient religious beliefs and various philosophies and systems of ethics – the means by which people in all ages have tried to answer the great universal questions. The plays are not intended to tell candidates what to think but to encourage them to examine how the great thinkers and civilizations of the past have approached these questions. One candidate is brought out of the audience and onto the stage as a stand-in for the rest, who only become involved when they are asked to rise all together, give the proper secret sign, and recite the oath for that degree.

You do not have to pass through the various degrees in order; in fact to attain the Thirty-second Degree you do not have to pass through Degrees Four to Thirty-one at all. The Thirty-third Degree is conferred by invitation only, and is awarded to members who have performed great services to Freemasonry, to the Scottish Rite, or to the community at large.

Benjamin Franklin at the opening of a Masonic lodge.

The growth of Freemasonry in the colonies was facilitated by the British army, whose lodges moved from place to place with the regiments. Officers would invite the local gentry to join, and when the regiment moved on the locals would establish a lodge of their own, applying to the Provincial Grand Master who under authority from the London Grand Lodge had the power to establish lodges in the colonies. Franklin remained an active and enthusiastic Freemason throughout his life, though thirty of those years were spent abroad, in London where he served as chief spokesman for the American colonies before the revolution and in Paris as ambassador to France once the War of Independence had broken out. He was a printer, publisher, writer, scientist and inventor; he was also president of Pennsylvania, postmaster general under the Continental Congress, and one of the committee of five that drafted the Declaration of Independence. When he returned from France after the success of the war against Britain, he was hailed by Americans as a champion of independence second only to General Washington. Yet when he died in 1790, and though twenty thousand Philadelphians filled the streets to watch the funeral procession, 'greater than ever was known on like occasion', and though the dignitaries included the clergy of the city, the assembly of the state, the Society of the Cincinnati and members of the American Philosophical Society, the city's Freemasonry lodges entirely ignored the event. By 1790, 59 years after he first joined a lodge, Benjamin Franklin had become, in the eyes of the Philadelphia brothers, the wrong kind of Freemason.

ANCIENTS AND MODERNS: CLASH OF CLASS

The explanation for this strange turn of events lies in the rise of the Ancients, a newly formed group of London Freemasons who in 1751 founded the Ancient Grand Lodge in direct opposition to the

Masonic Hall (Grand Lodge) Philadelphia (1812): though the 'Moderns' were the first to establish Freemasonry in Philadelphia, by 1790 the Ancients and their Temples, such as this one, had superseded them.

original Grand Lodge established since 1717. By 1757 the Ancients had founded a lodge in Philadelphia, and by Franklin's death in 1790 they had entirely taken over Freemasonry in Pennsylvania and would soon do so throughout the United States.

The Ancients in London were formed largely of Irishmen who described themselves as 'Men of some Education and an Honest Character but in low Circumstances'; they were recent immigrants to England who were often working in subsistence jobs, though they also found support among native English working people. Taken all together, these were a people whose financial and social circumstances made them uncomfortable with the gentrified nature of the original Grand Lodge; instead they wanted to reconnect Freemasonry to its artisan roots. Because they saw themselves as the upholders of the true and ancient traditions of Freemasonry, they called themselves the Ancients, and they attacked and attempted to undermine the members of the original Grand Lodge by calling them the Moderns.

Their *Book of Constitutions*, otherwise called the *Ahiman Rezon* (the title was supposedly Hebrew but in fact it has no meaning), was written by Laurence Dermott, an Irish journeyman painter, and published in 1756. It mocked the history section of Anderson's *Constitutions*, and answered it with a satirical chronology of its own which made the political point that many of the great men of history had started life in low circumstances. The *Ahiman Rezon* also inclined towards established Christianity and rejected Deism: 'A Mason is obliged by his Tenure to believe firmly in the true Worship of the eternal God, as well as in all those sacred Records which the Dignitaries and Fathers of the Church have compiled and published for the Use of all good Men: So that no one who rightly understands the Art, can possibly tread in the irreligious Paths of the unhappy Libertine, or be induced to follow the arrogant Professors of Atheism or Deism.'

In England the breach between the Ancients and the Moderns lasted 62 years; in 1813, after four years of negotiations and standardizing their rituals, procedures and regalia, they came together as the United Grand Lodge of England which continues to this day.

But matters progressed differently in America. One reason was the War of Independence. As the story of Benjamin Franklin shows, it would be wrong to say that Moderns were Loyalists and Ancients were for the revolution. What really happened was that with the revolution the entire nature of American society changed. Colonial Freemasonry had focused on teaching the arts and manners that would promote the solidarity of a genteel society; it encouraged the love and fellowship that would hold that society together. But the revolutionary mood attacked the notion of a society based on gentility and hierarchy. The Moderns belonged to a passing world; the new Freemasonry of America, the Freemasonry of its army, which was the Freemasonry of the Ancients, better represented a republican society of independent citizens proclaiming liberty and equality. By the time the war was over and Benjamin Franklin returned to America, the Moderns and their Lodges had ceased to exist. Franklin had become a 'Modern' Freemason without a home.

THE AMERICAN REVOLUTION

In the United States there has been a well-established legend that the Freemasons were behind the American Revolution. They are said to have instigated violent resistance to the British and to have defied British attempts to impose taxation without representation by holding the Boston Tea Party in 1773. It's also said that they drew up the Declaration of Independence in 1776, provided the leadership during the Revolutionary War, and drafted the Constitution in 1787.

But the role of the Freemasons has been exaggerated. A few Freemasons may have participated in the Boston Tea Party in 1773, but it was planned and executed by a group of radical artisans called the Sons of Liberty. Of the Committee of Five who drew up the Declaration of Independence, only two, Benjamin Franklin and Robert Livingston, were Freemasons, and the Declaration was almost entirely written by Thomas Jefferson, who was not a Freemason. Of the 55 Americans who signed the Declaration of

Independence, only 9 were certainly Freemasons; and of the 39 who approved the Constitution, only 13 were or later became Freemasons (not 'over a half', as Dan Brown writes in chapter 6 of *The Lost Symbol*). George Washington had become a Freemason at the age of twenty but did not take it seriously, regarding his lodge as a social club and showing up for only two meetings in the next 41 years. Just as at least a third of the American population remained loyal to the Crown, so did many American Freemasons. Benedict Arnold, who won the first great battle of the revolutionary war for the Americans at Saratoga, and who then defected to the British (so that in America his name is synonymous with treason), was a Freemason.

Yet in 1793, at the dedication of the Capitol Building, George Washington, in his capacity as first president of the United States, but wearing his Freemason's apron, placed a silver plate upon the foundation stone and covered it with the Masonic symbols of maize, oil and wine. An inscription on the silver plate made the identification of the new republic with Masonry absolutely clear: the stone had been laid, it stated, 'in the thirteenth year of American independence, and in the year of Masonry, 5793' – that being the generally accepted number of years since God's creation of the world. After the successful conclusion of the War of Independence, and for a generation after, Freemasonry was widely considered to be the foundation stone of the republic. The explanation lies in the creation of the revolutionary army with Washington at its head.

Washington had been initiated into Freemasonry in Fredericksburg, Virginia. As it happens, his lodge never had formal ties with the Grand Lodge of England, and a few years later, in 1758, when it finally received its charter, it was granted by the Grand Lodge of Scotland, an unofficial ally of the Ancient Grand Lodge in London. Washington's officers had been thrown together from a diversity of regional origins, religions and social ranks, and had great responsibilities thrust upon them. Freemasonry had been popular among officers in the British army in North America, who increasingly were Ancients, not Moderns. The revolutionary army continued the practice of having military lodges, usually following the Ancients' model, which it turned to good account. The Ancients' lack of social distinction, combined with Freemasonry's ideals of honour and fraternity, offered American officers the bonds on which to build the camaraderie necessary for the survival of the army, and therefore of the American republic.

MASONIC MURDERERS IN AMERICA?

Freemasonry had come to America from England, and been introduced to the colonial gentry, who used it to share Enlightenment ideas and genteel manners and pursuits among themselves, and to shape society in their image. But the revolution challenged the colonial social and political hierarchy, and a new form of Freemasonry, that of the Ancients who challenged the Moderns' status quo, epitomized the new nation. In the decades after independence, Freemasonry in the United States grew by leaps and bounds, and following the precedent of President Washington at the Capitol, hardly a church or university or public building had its cornerstone laid without a Masonic ceremony. Freemasonry represented the hopes and intentions of an enlightened republic, even as its citizens were having to adapt to a fast-changing and competitive environment with huge movements of people and vastly enlarged commercial activity within ever-expanding frontiers. But its secrecy on the one hand and its Enlightenment values on the other, together with suggestions of privilege and arrogance, brought Freemasonry into conflict with the increasingly populist, evangelical and conservative nature of American society.

The explosion came in 1826 with the disappearance of a man called William Morgan in the remote town of Batavia in upstate

New York. Morgan was a disgruntled Freemason who publicly threatened to publish a book that would reveal the secrets of the Craft. He was abducted by local Freemasons, and several days later a body found in the Niagara River was declared to be his. In the event, his wife denied that it was Morgan, while another

Morgan's kidnapping and presumed murder became a cause célèbre in the press and a rallying point for anti-Masonic feeling. His status as a martyr was also honoured in 1882 by an imposing monument in Batavia, New York state, erected by the National Christian Association. (This image is from an 1885 book by Léo Taxil – see p.70.)

woman identified the corpse as that of her own husband. The men who kidnapped Morgan said they took him to the Canadian border, put him on a horse, gave him $500, and told him never to come back. Others said the kidnappers had admitted tying Morgan's legs with weights and drowning him in the Niagara River. The men were tried, though none of them on murder charges, and they received only very light sentences. What really happened to William Morgan has never been known, though it does seem likely that he was killed.

What turned the case into a sensation was the discovery that the trial prosecutor and several of the jurors were Freemasons, and that in addition to the abductors themselves, a large number of other people, some working for the government, and all of them Freemasons, had colluded in the kidnapping. Suddenly it seemed that the Freemasons controlled the courts and the law enforcement bodies, and influenced the entire workings of New York State. What's more, it appeared that, having ritually murdered William Morgan, they had now used their vast network of brothers to protect their own.

Over the following weeks, months and years the outrage grew. At a New York political convention in 1828, a speaker demanded to know 'For what purpose have two thousand lodges been organized in these United States? Why are six hundred thousand men united together by mysterious ties, the nature of which are studiously concealed from their countrymen?' And as thousands of Freemasons renounced their membership, one condemned his former brethren by asking, 'Have they a longing for the faded liveries of the rotten aristocracies of Europe? Or, is it to prepare us for slavery that they have introduced the lordly names of "Most Worshipful", of "Knights", of "Kings" and "High Priests?"' And still twenty years after Morgan's disappearance, John Quincy Adams, the former president of the United States, condemned the Freemasons for rituals that involved dressing up as Knights Templar and drinking wine from human skulls.

These strange titles and rituals had grown out of Andrew Michael Ramsay's introduction of a fantastical Freemasonry to France. Over a thousand different ceremonies had been created since that time, mostly by the French. Some were taken up by the Ancients in Britain who introduced them to America; others arrived independently and were eventually grouped into the system of higher degrees known as the York Rite, while others formed the Scottish Rite. (Dan Brown makes no mention of the York Rite in *The Lost Symbol*, but it was big in early-nineteenth-century America and continues to this day, though it is outshone by the Scottish Rite.)

Post-revolutionary America was a world where social distinctions were forever being churned by change, and it may be that Americans craved whatever pomp and pageantry they could salvage. Perhaps the relentless shifting of American life also created a need for a secret world where the private self could rest and indulge a sense of history and meaning. What is certain is that nowhere in the world did Michael Andrew Ramsay's fantasy of Masonic chivalry take hold with such enthusiasm as in the United States. But 25 years after the founding of the Scottish Rite in South Carolina in 1801, American Freemasonry, with its pretensions to representing national values, was humbled by the outcry over the Morgan affair. From being the cornerstone of the republic, an institution regarded with the greatest respect and even awe, Freemasonry was revealed to inhabit a world of secret and suspect fantasies that seemed to undermine the American values of equality and democracy, and to undermine Christian values too. Tens of thousands of brothers turned their backs on the Craft, and lodges closed or went underground. Freemasonry in America all but collapsed.

ALBERT PIKE AND THE SCOTTISH RITE: THE SECRET WORLD WITHIN

Albert Pike, the 'Masonic luminary' mentioned by Dan Brown in *The Lost Symbol* (chapter 121), almost single-handedly restored the fortunes and vastly extended the popularity of Freemasonry in the second half of the nineteenth century. 'He found the organization in a log cabin and left it in a palace', wrote Manly Palmer Hall, the mystic philosopher whom Dan Brown quotes in the epigraph to *The Lost Symbol* and again in chapter 133. Hall called Pike 'the Platonic philosopher, the Hermetist, the alchemist, the Cabalist, and the transcendentalist', and went on to describe his esoteric researches: 'In his interpretation of Masonic symbolism, Albert Pike naturally turned, as all scholars must ultimately do, to those ancient institutions of learning from which has descended to this age the whole bounty of rational good. Nor does Pike hesitate, through any false pride, to acknowledge the origin of his illumination. In the Mysteries of Ceres and Proserpine at Eleusis, of Isis and Osiris in Egypt, of Atys and Adonis in Syria, of the Druses in Lebanon and the Druids of Britain, of the persecuted Gnostics and the reviled Cabalists, as well as a score of others, he found the roots of that great tree which was to grow up through the ages under the name of Freemasonry and spread its branches over the modern world.'

Albert Pike's statue stands in Washington, DC, the inscription reading 'philanthropist, philosopher, jurist, orator, author, poet, scholar, soldier', though as the Smithsonian Institution's own newsletter has suggested, for the sake of accuracy the words 'libertine, traitor, glutton, incompetent, murderer' should be added. Born in Boston, Massachusetts, in 1809, Pike was a self-made man who claimed he went to Harvard and left for lack of money, though no record of his attendance can be found. Self-taught in classics and poetry, he spoke French, Latin, ancient Greek and Hebrew, and after the age of seventy taught himself Sanskrit too. In his twenties he went west, travelled through the Mexican territories and eventually settled in Arkansas, where he trained himself in law and acted for Native American tribes in their claims against the United States government. When the Civil War broke out, and despite his Northern birth, Pike served as a brigadier general in the Confederate army, leading a battalion of Native Americans against the Northern forces. His men were accused of scalping and defiling the Union dead, and Pike was forced to resign; he was also imprisoned when his fellow officers charged him with misappropriating funds.

After the war Pike abandoned his wife and eleven children in Arkansas and travelled throughout the country, practising law, editing a newspaper, writing poetry and reputedly creating the rituals of the Ku Klux Klan. In 1868 he settled in Washington, DC, where he began an affair with the vivacious nineteen-year-old sculptress Vinnie Ream, forty years his junior. Her marble statues of Abraham Lincoln, completed when she was 21, and of the Indian chief Sequoyah stand in the Capitol Building's Statuary Hall. Pike himself cut quite a figure, according to a contemporary. 'A giant in body, in brain, in heart and in soul. So majestic in appearance that whenever he moved on highway or byway, the wide world over, every passer-by turned to gaze upon him and admire him. Six feet, two inches, with the proportions of a Hercules and the grace of an Apollo. A face and head massive and leonine, recalling in every feature some sculptor's dream of a Grecian god; while his long wavy hair, flowing down over his shoulders, added a striking picturesque effect.'

In the year that he took up with Ream, Pike rewrote all the rituals of the Scottish Rite, from the fourth to the thirty-second degree, and he followed this in 1871 with the publication of *Morals and Dogma* (see box overleaf), his vast commentary on the rituals of the three Craft degrees and the twenty-nine higher degrees.

Pike returned to the example of James Anderson's *Constitutions*, which traced a line from Solomon's masons via Greece and Rome to show that modern Freemasonry was the inheritor of the arcane knowledge and esoteric secrets of the ancient world. 'Masonry is identical with the ancient Mysteries', Pike declared in that chapter of *Morals and Dogma* dealing with initiation into the Second Degree, a message repeated and illustrated on every page. But he had nothing to say about Freemasonry's role in shaping American

FROM MORALS AND DOGMA TO THE LOST SYMBOL

Albert Pike wrote *Morals and Dogma* as a commentary on the degrees of the Scottish Rite, those very degrees which he himself had revised. In his preface to the book, Pike wrote that 'dogma' was meant in the sense of teaching; he was not laying down the law, only asking his readers to 'weigh what is taught'. Presumably the Supreme Council of the Scottish Rite, Southern Jurisdiction, did weigh the contents of Pike's book and found that it possessed moral and instructive value, as for over a hundred years, until 1974, they gave a free copy to every candidate who advanced as far as the Fourteenth Degree.

Pike was convinced that the Scottish Rite degrees were part of a primitive Masonry that had preserved something of the Ancient Mysteries that had been known to Egypt, Asia Minor and ancient Greece. But mere Craft Masonry, he said, was blind to those Mysteries. In fact, he went further and claimed that the three degrees of Craft Masonry had been invented for the specific purpose of hiding the truth of this deeper learning. As Pike wrote in *Morals and Dogma*, 'The Blue Degrees are but the outer court or portico of the Temple. Part of the symbols are displayed there to the Initiate, but he is intentionally misled by false interpretations. It is not intended that he shall understand them; but it is intended that he shall imagine he understands them. Their true explication is reserved for the Adepts, the Princes of Masonry.'

Sublime Prince of the Royal Secret was the original title given to those who achieved the Thirty-second Degree in the Scottish Rite, though the title is now more democratically rendered as Master of the Royal Secret. The opening paragraph of Pike's chapter on the Thirty-second Degree catches the flavour of his writing: 'The Occult Science of the Ancient Magi was concealed under the shadows of the Ancient Mysteries: it was imperfectly revealed or rather disguised by the Gnostics: it is guessed at under the obscurities that cover the pretended crimes of the Templars; and it is found enveloped in enigmas that seem impenetrable, in the Rites of the Highest Masonry.'

society; it seemed safer to look inwards and at most embrace a vague ethical symbolism. By 1884 the number of brothers well exceeded that of 1826 but, as Pike himself admitted, Freemasonry had regained its membership at the expense of the leadership and example that had previously allowed it to command the awed respect due to an institution at the centre of society. The proof was that the newly popular Freemasonry of the late nineteenth century failed to attract serious attack.

The original edition of *Morals and Dogma*, published in 1871, was over a thousand pages long and without the index amounted to 861 pages of text. A good half of this, as Pike freely admitted in his preface, was taken from other sources, but he did not say what those sources were. Certainly parts of *Morals and Dogma* were lifted from the writings of Eliphas Lévi, a French occultist and magician, who saved himself the trouble of exhaustive research by making things up. Lévi was briefly a Freemason and claimed that Masonic symbolism was borrowed from the Kabbalah, but when he was challenged to give proof, he walked out of his lodge and never returned. But Pike was uncritical and swallowed Lévi's claims whole. And they went far beyond the Kabbalah, Lévi finding the origins for Freemasonry also in Gnosticism, Zoroastrianism, Brahmanism, alchemy and Egyptian mysticism.

With his knowledge of French, Pike was able to read what was probably Levi's greatest work, *Dogme et Rituel de la Haute Magie,* published in France in 1854 (translated into English in 1896 as *Transcendental Magic: Its Doctrine and Ritual*). In this book Lévi set out the essence of occult belief in one grand sweeping sentence: 'Behind the veil of all the hieratic and mystical allegories of ancient doctrines, behind the darkness and strange ordeals of all initiations, under the seal of all sacred writings, in the ruins of Nineveh or Thebes, on the crumbling stones of old temples and on the blackened visage of the Assyrian or Egyptian sphinx, in the monstrous or marvellous paintings which interpret to the faithful of India the inspired pages of the Vedas, in the cryptic emblems of our old books on alchemy, in the ceremonies practised at reception by all secret societies, there are found indications of a doctrine which is everywhere the same and everywhere carefully concealed.'

This story of hidden mysteries waiting to be revealed formed the basis of Albert Pike's *Morals and Dogma*, and it is also the theme of Dan Brown's *The Lost Symbol*.

Albert Pike, '... some sculptor's dream of a Grecian god'.

For the last 32 years of his life Pike was the Sovereign Grand Master of the Thirty-third Degree for the Southern Jurisdiction of the United States. He died in 1891; his bronze statue in Judiciary Square, the only outdoor statue of a Confederate officer in Washington, DC, was raised in 1901; and when the House of the Temple, the great headquarters of the Scottish Rite modelled after the original Mausoleum, was completed in 1915, Pike's remains were interred there.

FREEMASONRY IN THE MODERN WORLD

The twentieth century saw Freemasonry coming face to face with new social and political realities in Britain, the country of its founding; in the United States, where it was enjoying a renewed popularity; and on the continent of Europe, which was entering a terrible period of conflict. The same was true elsewhere in the world.

The generally liberal climate of Britain and America and the assured safeguard of the rule of law, together with the policy within lodges of not discussing politics or religion, has done much to keep Freemasonry at a distance from controversy. In both countries, however, there has been the question of whether membership should be extended to women. One argument against it has been that wives are better off having their husbands attending an all-male organization than a mixed one with its opportunities for hanky-panky; it is an argument that has found favour with both men and women. Separate women's lodges have been established in Britain and the United States, and also in Canada, France, Belgium, Italy and other countries. The women-only Honourable Fraternity of Ancient Freemasons has over 350 lodges in Great Britain and is recognized by the United Grand Lodge of England, though no Masonic contact takes place between them. Similarly there is the Ancient and Primitive Rite of Memphis-Misraïm, one of several women-only groups recognized by Grand Lodges in the United States. (The Order of the Eastern Star, a largely American organization mentioned several times by Dan Brown in *The Lost Symbol* as a female equivalent of Freemasonry, does not confer the three Craft degrees but follows its own rituals and is not recognized as Freemasonry by the Grand Lodges in the United States, though most do give it their blessing.)

Another matter in the United States has been race. A history of segregation led to the creation of the parallel all-black Prince Hall lodges, named for the son of an English soldier and a black African mother who was born in Boston and was accepted into a British military lodge there in 1775. Prince Hall lodges are recognized by most other lodges in America, and also in recent decades there has been a degree of mixing, with blacks joining previously all-white lodges and whites joining all-black lodges.

On the continent of Europe Freemasonry was faced with the new communist and fascist regimes. When the Bolsheviks came

to power in 1917 Freemasonry was banned throughout the Soviet Union. Freemasonry was also banned in Italy when Mussolini came to power in 1922, and it was banned in Germany when Hitler came to power in 1934, the minister of the interior saying it was 'inapproriate that a secret society with obscure aims should continue to exist in the Third Reich'. The suppression of Freemasonry was extended wherever fascist or communist governments came to power in Europe during the twentieth

The forget-me-not flower became a secret badge of fraternity for Freemasons in Nazi Germany. After 1945 it became an official emblem of Freemasonry in Germany.

century, including Spain, Portugal, France and Eastern Europe. Freemasons were rounded up in Vichy France during World War II, with the Vichy leader Marshal Pétain, a Catholic, saying that Freemasons were worse than Jews because a Jew was born a Jew but a Freemason chose to be a Freemason. A thousand French Freemasons were sent to German concentration camps where over half were executed or died from the terrible conditions.

Following the collapse of these fascist and communist regimes, Freemasonry is now freely organized across Europe. But during the twentieth century Freemasonry also found itself facing two other problems. One has been the growth of lurid conspiracy theories that place Freemasonry at the centre of every conceivable and inconceivable plot and movement in the world. Some case might have been made for Freemasons playing important roles in the American and French revolutions (though there were plenty of Freemasons who opposed those revolutions too), and the powerful reaction to the Morgan affair in the early decades of the United States was at least based on some strong indications that Freemasons were abusing their positions of trust. But modern-day attacks on Freemasonry have no basis in reality whatsoever, and the conspiracies raised against them are wholly imaginary. Complementary to these conspiracy charges has been modern anti-Semitism, which exists independently of anti-Freemasonry but is also combined with fantasies about Freemasonry to turn it into an organization controlled by Jews with a secret Jewish-inspired worldwide agenda.

Freemasons seem to find enemies in absolutist systems and among organizations that make a claim to universal dominion. These have included fascists and communists, but also various Protestant denominations, the Roman Catholic Church and Islam, as discussed below. To the absolutist and dogmatic mind, the secrecy of Freemasonry can be taken as defiance or subversion or godlessness, and not a little anti-Semitism is often a factor.

Opposite: an idol of Baphomet carried in a procession at the initiation of a high Scottish rite. The image is from a lurid 1885 book, *Les Mystères de la Franc Maçonnerie*, by serial hoaxer Léo Taxil. Taxil may have been motivated by an opportunity to ingratiate himself with the Catholic Church – the target of a previous slander.

Anti-Masonic feeling received a big boost from Taxil's sensational revelations of a secret, erotically charged and Devil-worshipping Masonic order, the Palladium. Deliberately misquoting Albert Pike as 'proof' of the Freemasons' support of Luciferian doctrine, Taxil was reviving an old tradition which linked the Knights Templar with devil worship, updating it for their supposed heirs the Freemasons. Taxil confessed to his fabrications twelve years later at a public lecture from which he had to flee pursued by an angry crowd, but inevitably some of the mud stuck.

ANTI-MASONRY AND RELIGION

Dan Brown sees Freemasonry as 'a global organization that is spiritual and yet will bring Muslims, Jews, Christians and even just people who are confused about religion – bring them together'. But that is not the way much of the world sees Freemasonry.

With varying degrees of intensity, a number of Protestant denominations around the world, including Baptists, Methodists, Anglicans and Quakers, discourage their congregants from becoming Freemasons.

The head of the Anglican Church, Rowan Williams, the Archbishop of Canterbury, has stated his 'real misgivings about the compatibility of Masonry and Christian profession' and has admitted that when still a bishop he blocked the appointment of Freemasons to senior positions. The Anglican Synod in Sydney, Australia, has declared that Freemasonry and Christianity are 'fundamentally and irreconcilably incompatible' and that Freemasonry 'teaches and upholds a system of false religious and spiritual beliefs that are contrary to biblical Christianity'. A two-year study by the Assembly of the Church of Scotland found 'very real theological difficulties' with Freemasonry. The Methodist Conference in England has said that Freemasonry competes with Christian beliefs, has banned

Masonic meetings on Methodist premises, and has asked Methodist Freemasons to reconsider their membership in the Craft.

All of which is mild compared to the opposition to Freemasonry by the Roman Catholic Church and Islam, whose followers amount to about half the world's population.

Roman Catholics have been prohibited from becoming Freemasons since 1738. The Vatican has restated its position over the years in a number of papal bulls which punish membership of Freemasonry with excommunication. The most recent of these, *Humanum Genus*, was promulgated by Pope Leo XIII in 1884. Its central theme was that, with the rise of industrialism and secularism, the late nineteenth century was a dangerous era for Christians, and it particularly condemned Freemasonry for its claim that the people were sovereign, that education should be the responsibility of the state, and that Church and state should be separated. These views, in rejecting the intervention of God in human affairs, were on the path towards Deism and Gnosticism and would lead to 'the kingdom of Satan'. The bull was reinforced by the Code of Canon Law promulgated in 1917 which said membership in Freemasonry meant automatic excommunication. An apparent softening of the Church's position came in 1974, when it declared that excommunication would no longer be automatic, but the most recent statement, emanating in 1983 from the Congregation for the Doctrine of the Faith headed by Cardinal Ratzinger (now Pope Benedict XVI), declared that 'The faithful who enroll in Masonic associations are in a state of grave sin and may not receive Holy Communion', and added that 'the Church's negative judgement in regard to Masonic association remains unchanged since their principles have always been considered irreconcilable with the doctrine of the Church and therefore membership in them remains forbidden'.

The Roman Catholic Church also forbids any writing on Freemasonry that is in any way sympathetic, but it does fulsomely

Cardinal Ratzinger, the future Pope Benedict XVI (standing), oversaw the Catholic Church's last statement on the 'grave sin' of Freemasonry in 1983.

RUDYARD KIPLING: COSMOPOLITAN FREEMASON

Rudyard Kipling, who was born in India in 1865, is most famous as the author of the novel *Kim* and of tales for children such as *The Jungle Book* and the *Just So Stories*. Kipling received the Nobel Prize for Literature in 1907. He became a Freemason when he was 23, and he fondly recalled the cosmopolitan character of his lodge when writing in *The Times* in 1925: 'I was Secretary for some years of Hope and Perseverance Lodge No. 782, E.C. Lahore which included Brethren of at least four creeds. I was entered by a member of Bramo Somaj, a Hindu; passed by a Mohammedan, and raised by an Englishman. Our Tyler was an Indian Jew. We met, of course, on the level, and the only difference anyone would notice was that at our banquets, some of the Brethren, who were debarred by caste from eating food not ceremonially prepared, sat over empty plates.'

Kipling wrote a poem called 'The Mother-Lodge' which celebrates the mix of backgrounds enjoyed by Freemasons in India at the time.

There was Rundle, Station Master,
An' Beazeley of the Rail,
An' 'Ackman, Commissariat,
An' Donkin' o' the Jail;
An' Blake, Conductor-Sargent,
Our Master twice was 'e,
With 'im that kept the Europe-shop,
Old Framjee Eduljee.

support and promote a book called *The Mystery of Freemasonry Unveiled* by José María Caro, the late Cardinal of Chile. First published in 1925, the book has been in print ever since, and is sold by Catholic bookshops around the world. Here, for example, is a summary of the book provided by the Angelus Press of Kansas City, Missouri, an online purveyor of Catholic works: 'This book remains the best summary and reference book on the deceits and evils of Masonry. Exposes the worldwide plans for the destruction of the Christian order, as well as its anti-Catholic fury throughout the world. Covers all aspects of Masonry, Satanic societies, the use of Masonry as an Instrument of Judaism and a resume of condemnations of Masonry by the Church. Focuses on principles, not con-

Outside – 'Sergeant! Sir! Salute! Salaam!'
Inside – 'Brother', an' it doesn't do no 'arm.
We met upon the Level an' we parted on the Square,
An' I was Junior Deacon in my Mother-Lodge out there!

We'd Bola Nath, Accountant,
An' Saul the Aden Jew,
An' Din Mohammed, draughtsman
Of the Survey Office too;
There was Babu Chuckerbutty,
An' Amir Singh the Sikh,
An' Castro from the fittin'-sheds,
The Roman Catholick!

We 'adn't good regalia,
An' our Lodge was old an' bare,
But we knew the Ancient Landmarks,
An' we kep' 'em to a hair;
An' lookin' on it backwards
It often strikes me thus,
There ain't such things as infidels,
Excep', per'aps, it's us.

spiracy theories. Highly recommended by Cardinals Benlloch and Billot. Many references. This is a classic!'

Islam is no less retiring in its condemnation of Freemasonry, which is banned almost everywhere in the Muslim world and is subject to severe punishments, including death. Among Muslim countries, only Malaysia, Bosnia-Herzegovina, Turkey and Morocco tolerate Freemasonry, and also Lebanon which is a half-Christian country.

Al-Azhar mosque and university in Cairo is the foremost centre of Islamic theology in the world; when the sheikhs at al-Azhar speak, the Muslim world listens and generally follows their directions. In 1978 al-Azhar's Islamic Jurisdictional College issued its views on Freemasonry:

After complete research concerning this organization, based on written accounts from many sources, we have determined...

1. Freemasonry is a clandestine organization, which conceals or reveals its system, depending on the circumstances. Its actual principles are hidden from members, except for chosen members of its higher degrees.

2. The members of the organization, worldwide, are drawn from men without preference for their religion, faith or sect.

3. The organization attracts members on the basis of providing personal benefits. It traps men into being politically active, and its aims are unjust.

4. New members participate in ceremonies of different names and symbols, and are frightened from disobeying its regulations and orders.

5. Members are free to practise their religion, but only members who are atheists are promoted to its higher degrees, based on how much they are willing to serve its dangerous principles and plans.

6. It is a political organization. It has served all revolutions, military and political transformations. In all dangerous changes a relation to this organization appears either exposed or veiled.

7. It is a Jewish organization in its roots. Its secret higher international administrative board are Jews and it promotes Zionist activities.

8. Its primary objectives are the distraction of all religions and it distracts Muslims from Islam.

9. It tries to recruit influential financial, political, social, or scientific people to utilize them. It does not consider applicants it cannot utilize. It recruits kings, prime ministers, high government officials and similar individuals.

10. It has branches under different names as a camouflage, so people cannot trace its activities, especially if the name of 'Freemasonry' has opposition. These hidden branches are known as Lions, Rotary and others. They have wicked principles that completely contradict the rules of Islam. There is a clear relationship between Freemasonry, Judaism and International Zionism. It has controlled the activities of high Arab officials in the Palestinian problem. It has limited their duties, obligations and activities for the benefit of Judaism and International Zionism.

And the report concludes: 'Given that Freemasonry involves itself in dangerous activities, it is a great hazard, with wicked objectives, the Jurisdictional Synod determines that Freemasonry is a dangerous, destructive organization. Any Muslim who affiliates with it, knowing the truth of its objectives, is an infidel to Islam.'

SOME NOTABLE FREEMASONS

The following is a selection of notable Freemasons from various walks of life.

THE BRITISH ROYAL FAMILY

George IV
William IV
Edward VII
Edward VIII
George VI
Prince Philip, Duke of Edinburgh, husband of Queen Elizabeth II

PRESIDENTS OF THE UNITED STATES

George Washington
James Monroe
Andrew Jackson
James Polk
James Buchanan
Andrew Johnson
James Garfield
William McKinley
Theodore Roosevelt
William Howard Taft
Warren Harding
Franklin Roosevelt
Harry Truman
Gerald Ford

PUBLIC FIGURES

Philip Wharton, 1st Duke of Wharton, early-eighteenth-century English politician, atheist and libertine

Giacomo Casanova, eighteenth-century Venetian adventurer and lover

Chevalier D'Eon de Beaumont, eighteenth-century French diplomat and transsexual

Benjamin Franklin, publisher, writer, American revolutionary and statesman

Paul Revere, silversmith and American revolutionary

John Hancock, American revolutionary, merchant and statesman

Marquis de Lafayette, French general, statesman and supporter of the American Revolution

Edmund Burke, eighteenth-century British parliamentarian, supporter of the American Revolution and an opponent of the French Revolution

Jean-Paul Marat, eighteenth-century French revolutionary

Montgolfier brothers, Jacques-Étienne and Joseph-Michel, eighteenth-century French inventors and pilots of the first hot air balloon

Adam Weishaupt, late-eighteenth- and early-nineteenth-century German philosopher and founder of the Order of the Illuminati

Thomas Stamford Raffles, early-nineteenth-century British statesman and founder of Singapore

Símon Bolívar, nineteenth-century leader of South American independence

Davy Crockett, nineteenth-century American frontiersman, soldier and politician

John Brown, American mid-nineteenth-century abolitionist ▶

NOTABLE FREEMASONS CONTINUED

Sir Richard Burton, nineteenth-century British explorer, soldier, diplomat and translator of the *Kama Sutra*

Giuseppe Garibaldi, nineteenth-century Italian general and revolutionary who contributed towards the unification of Italy

Sheikh Mohammed Abdu, late-nineteenth-century Egyptian cleric at Cairo's al-Azhar mosque and university, also a nationalist and a religious and cultural reformer

Saad Zaghloul, early-twentieth-century Egyptian nationalist and prime minister

Mustafa Kemal Ataturk, founder of the modern Republic of Turkey

Charles Lindbergh, American aviator and politician

Winston Churchill, British prime minister

J. Edgar Hoover, head of the FBI

Sir Robert Menzies, Australia's longest-serving prime minister, mid-twentieth century

Geoffrey Fisher, mid-twentieth-century Archbishop of Canterbury and head of the worldwide Anglican Communion

Earl Warren, Chief Justice of the United States, 1953–69

Salvador Allende, socialist president of Chile, early 1970s

John Glenn, astronaut and US senator

Jesse Jackson, American civil rights leader and politician

MILITARY FIGURES

Benedict Arnold, American Revolutionary War general, victor at the battle of Saratoga, but ultimately a traitor to the cause

Duke of Wellington, British general in the Napoleonic wars, victor at Waterloo

Horatio Nelson, British admiral in the Napoleonic wars, victor in the battle of Trafalgar

Lord Kitchener, late-nineteenth- and early-twentieth-century British general, victor in the battle of Omdurman

John J. Pershing, general commanding the American Expeditionary Force in France during World War I

General Douglas MacArthur, American commander in the Pacific, World War II

THE PERFORMING ARTS

Count Basie, jazz orchestra leader and composer

Irving Berlin, composer

Duke Ellington, jazz musician

Nat King Cole, pianist and singer

Cecil B. DeMille, film director

Harry Houdini, escape artist

W.C. Fields, actor and comedian

Clark Gable, actor

John Wayne, actor

Harpo Marx, actor and comedian

Peter Sellers, actor and comedian

William 'Bud' Abbott, the thin half of the Abbott and Costello comedy team

Oliver Hardy, the fat half of Laurel and Hardy

Art, Architecture, Literature

Elias Ashmole, seventeenth-century English antiquary whose collection of manuscripts formed the basis of the Ashmolean Library, Oxford

Christopher Wren, English architect who built St Paul's Cathedral

Jonathan Swift, Anglo-Irish cleric and writer, author of *Gulliver's Travels*

William Hogarth, eighteenth-century English painter, cartoonist and satirist

Edward Gibbon, eighteenth-century English historian, author of *The Decline and Fall of the Roman Empire*

Voltaire, French philosopher and reformer whose writings influenced the American and French revolutions; he was made a Freemason by Benjamin Franklin

James Boswell, eighteenth-century Scottish writer and biographer of Dr Johnson

Wolfgang Amadeus Mozart, Austrian composer whose works include several pieces of Masonic ritual music and the Masonic opera *The Magic Flute*

Sir John Soane, late-eighteenth- and early-nineteenth-century English architect and collector of antiquities; his home and collection are now the Sir John Soane Museum, London

Robert Burns, Scottish poet

Johann Wolfgang von Goethe, German philosopher and poet

William Hoban Irish-born architect of the White House.

Alexander Pushkin, nineteenth-century poet, considered to be Russia's greatest

Mark Twain, American novelist

Alexandre Gustav Eiffel, French engineer and designer of the Eiffel Tower; he also built the armature for the Statue of Liberty

Frédéric Bartholdi, French sculptor and designer of the Statue of Liberty

Sir Arthur Sullivan, half of Gilbert and Sullivan

Sir W.S. Gilbert, the other half of Gilbert and Sullivan

Sir Arthur Conan Doyle, British novelist and creator of Sherlock Holmes

Alphonse Mucha, Czech art nouveau artist

Oscar Wilde, Irish playwright, novelist and poet

Rudyard Kipling, British writer and poet, Nobel Prize winner

Marc Chagall, Russian artist

Aleister Crowley, English occultist, hedonist and social critic, called 'the wickedest man in the world'

Manly Palmer Hall, Canadian-born esoteric author

▶

NOTABLE FREEMASONS CONTINUED

Sir P.G. Wodehouse, English writer and humorist, author of the Jeeves stories

Billy Wilder, American filmmaker, screenwriter and producer

SCIENCE AND MEDICINE

Edward Jenner, late-eighteenth-century English pioneer of the smallpox vaccine

Dr Joseph Guillotin, inventor of the guillotine

Joseph Lister, nineteenth-century English surgeon who pioneered the use of antiseptics

Sir Alexander Fleming, twentieth-century Scottish biologist and pharmacologist, who won the Nobel Prize for his discovery of penicillin

BUSINESS

John Jacob Astor, built his fortune on late-eighteenth-century fur trading activities; when he died in 1848 he was the richest man in the United States

Nathan Meyer Rothschild, nineteenth-century British financier

Henry Ford, founder of the Ford Motor Company

Horace Saks, founder of Saks Fifth Avenue

André Citroen, French engineer and motor car manufacturer

Walter Chrysler, founder of the Chrysler Corporation

Colonel Harland Sanders, founder of the Kentucky Fried Chicken fast food chain

Steve Wozniak, co-founder with Steve Jobs of Apple Computers

Good apple? Philanthropist and co-founder of Apple Computers Steve Wozniak was initiated into the Freemasons in 1980.

The Mysteries

KNOW YE NOT THAT YE ARE GODS?

'"The secret hides within" was the core tenet of the mysteries, urging mankind to seek God *not* in the heavens above ... but rather within himself. *The secret hides within.* It was the message of all the great mystical teachers.
The kingdom of God is within you, said Jesus Christ.
Know thyself, said Pythagoras.
Know ye not that ye are gods, said Hermes Trismegistus.
The list went on and on...'

THE LOST SYMBOL [CHAPTER 102]

In *The Da Vinci Code*, Dan Brown challenged the fundamental assertions of the Christian story. In *The Lost Symbol*, he challenges the underpinnings of our entire world view. Mainstream Western culture has been based on the two pillars of faith and reason, on the Christianity of the churches on the one hand, and on philosophical rationalism on the other. These two principles, reason and faith, have sometimes been in opposition to one another, but generally they have coexisted, if in separate spheres, since the seventeenth century and the birth of the Age of Reason, when science and philosophy were detached from theology.

Christianity goes back two thousand years, while the Western tradition of rational inquiry goes back even further, to ancient Greek philosophy. But quite different from the two, and ignored by both when not actively suppressed, has been a third element that has existed in certain phases and corners of our culture: a belief that experience is prime, that what matters above all else is our direct apprehension of the self and the divine. This gnosis, as it has been called, a 'knowing', has nothing to do with doctrine or dogma, nor with institutions or proofs: it is the sensation you get when you look up at the stars and at the same time survey your own being, your mind, your feelings, your pulsating heart, and come to the realization that human beings are in their deepest essence at one with divine reality – 'as above, so below', as Hermes Trismegistus (see p.100) said.

This is what Dan Brown is saying in *The Lost Symbol*, that there is a missing element in our world, a third way, and that we must look again at the experience of the ancients, and what they had to say, look again at philosophers such as Pythagoras, at prophets such as Jesus, at the works of the Hermeticists and the lives of the Gnostics, and at the Ancient Mysteries of Greece, Rome and Egypt. They all have one thing in common, says Dan Brown: they all carry the realization that we are gods.

THE MYSTERIES OF APHRODITE AND ADONIS

The Mysteries of the ancient world were religious cults, whose rituals were a fiercely guarded secret, known only to the initiated. 'Mysteries' comes from the Greek word *mysteria*, meaning secret, and ultimately from the verb *myo*, meaning to keep one's mouth shut. Isis and Osiris of Egypt, Cybele and Attis of Asia Minor, Aphrodite and Adonis of Syria, Mythras of Persia, and Persephone and Dionysus of Greece, these were the gods at the heart of the great Mysteries of the ancient world. What they all had in common was the story of life and death followed by rebirth. Their outer myths were well known. But their inner drama, the one undergone by their initiates, was a mystery.

Like all the myths of the gods, the story of Adonis comes in various forms, but the best-known version is that told by the Greeks from the fifth century BC onwards. Adonis, goes the story, was born of the incestuous love encouraged by the goddess Aphrodite between King Cinyras of Byblos in Lebanon and his daughter. When the child was born, Aphrodite was taken by his unearthly beauty and hid him in a chest which she placed in the care of Persephone, queen of the underworld. But when Persephone opened the chest, she too was enchanted and wanted to keep the child for her own. Zeus was called in to mediate in this dispute between death and love, and decreed that Adonis must live part of each year with Persephone in the dismal underworld but during the other part could return to the shining world above. There Adonis and Aphrodite became lovers, exchanging their first kisses in a mountain cave, the source of a river that ran down to the sea at Byblos. But those kisses were also their last, for near the cave Adonis was gored by a wild boar, perhaps Ares, the jealous husband of Aphrodite, in disguise. Though Aphrodite tried to heal Adonis's wounds, he bled to death. Bright spring anemones grew where his blood touched the ground, and the river down to Byblos ran red.

Aphrodite is of course the Roman Venus. In her earlier Semitic form she was Astarte, and in Babylonia she was Ishtar, the great mother goddess who was the embodiment of the reproductive energies of nature. Ishtar's lover was Tammuz, who was addressed by his devotees as Adon ('lord'); this title was mistakenly taken by the Greeks to be his name – hence 'Adonis'. Tammuz was a vegetation god who every year was believed to die, his divine mistress journeying into the underworld in search of him. In her absence the passion of love ceased to operate in the upper world, men and animals forgot to procreate, and all life was threatened with extinction.

At Byblos, the principal centre of the Adonis cult, these were the days of lamentation: 'He is dead, Adonis the beautiful, he is dead!' Women would beat their breasts and shave their heads, and some offered themselves for sacred prostitution. Then on the eighth day the sorrow turned to rejoicing: 'He is risen, Adonis, he is risen!' These same celebrations were held all over the Eastern Mediterranean, in Cyprus, Athens and Alexandria. In Alexandria, Adonis was closely associated with the Egyptian Osiris, whom the Greeks in turn identified with their own Dionysus.

THE MYSTERIES OF OSIRIS AND ISIS

Following the conquests of Alexander the Great in the late fourth century BC, Greeks ruled vast kingdoms in the East, extending from the Mediterranean to India. Egypt was among them, ruled by the Ptolemies, a dynasty descended from one of Alexander's generals. The Greeks were great admirers of the Egyptians, whom they venerated for their antiquity and the wisdom of their priests, and already in the centuries before Alexander, when Greeks like the fifth-century historian Herodotus visited Egypt, they were fascinated by its culture, identified its gods with their own, and liked to believe that Egypt was the source of many of their own ceremonies and beliefs.

Herodotus described two huge festivals in the Delta, the most important in Egypt in his time, one in honour of Artemis at Bubastis, the other in honour of Isis at her vast temple in Busiris. 'They come in barges, men and women together, a great number in each boat', he wrote of the pilgrims travelling to the festival of Artemis. 'On the way, some of the women keep up a continual clatter with castinets and some of the men play flutes, while the rest, both men and women, sing and clap their hands. Whenever they pass a town on the riverbank, they bring the barge close inshore, some of the women continuing to act as I have said, while others shout abuse at the women of the place or start dancing, or stand up and hitch up their skirts. When they reach Bubastis they celebrate the festival with elaborate sacrifices, and more wine is consumed than during all the rest of the year. The numbers that meet there, are, according to a native report, as many as 700,000 men and women.' At the temple of Isis at Busiris the scenes were similar: 'It is here that everybody – tens of thousands of men and women – when the sacrifice is over, beat their breasts: in whose honour, however, I do not feel it is proper for me to say'. The god Herodotus will not mention is Osiris, the husband of Isis, and his reticence is probably due to the fact that a mystery performance linked to Osiris was taking place there at the time. The rituals of these mysteries were such a jealously guarded secret that even a passing allusion to them was taboo.

Osiris first appeared around 2350 BC inside the pyramid of Unas, the last king of the Fifth Dynasty in the Egypt of the Old Kingdom. Unusually, the pyramid's chamber walls, which are normally left undecorated, were this time covered in hieroglyphic inscriptions. These Pyramid Texts, the earliest extensive mortuary texts in Egypt, are in the form of prayers by the king who seeks to identify himself with Osiris. Previous kings had felt themselves to be gods, absolute in their powers; or their authority was shared with Ra, though the sun god was also a guarantor of their royal position. Egyptians knew God only through their king. Osiris, however, as lord of the underworld, performed the role of a judge who examined the souls of the dead and condemned those unfit for the afterlife – now, even the king must plead his case. With the rise of the cult of Osiris came the notion of a personal god from whom one sought redemption. Soon ordinary Egyptians were adapting the royal rituals to themselves, inscribing portions of the Pyramid Texts on their coffins, so that they too would achieve deification at death by becoming an Osiris.

Isis was introduced in those same Pyramid Texts as the sister and wife of Osiris. The texts relate how Osiris was killed by his brother Seth who dismembered the body. But Isis searched out the pieces and put them together again, wondrously restoring Osiris to life in the underworld, where he reigned as judge and king. Horus, the son of Isis by Osiris, was secretly raised to manhood and, after a long and desperate struggle, overcame Seth and established order all over Egypt. Mystically, Horus was the incarnation of his father, while Isis was the agent both of resurrection and of reincarnation. For the Egyptians, Osiris was central to the myth; he was their dead king and Horus was their living king.

But when the Greeks took over Egypt, they were keen to legitimize their rule by claiming that the mother of their kings was Isis. And so her importance grew, but not only for political reasons; ordinary people, Greeks and Egyptians, saw in the suffering and joy experienced by Isis at the death and resurrection of her husband something that was emotionally attractive and with which they could identify. So powerful and satisfying was the story of Isis that she became identified in turn with all the other goddesses of the Mediterranean, whom she finally absorbed. Isis was the Goddess of Ten Thousand Names, Shelter and Heaven to All Mankind, the House of Life, the Great Mother of All Gods and Nature, Victorious over Fate, the Goddess of Sexuality and the Promise of Immortality. She was passionately worshipped by men and women alike. Apuleius, the second-century author of the Latin proto-novel *Metamorphoses* (also known as *The Golden Ass*), described his initiation into the Mysteries of Isis as a deeply moving spiritual experience in which he suffered a mystic death and resurrection, and felt bound to the goddess for the rest of his life.

Long after Christianity became the official religion of the Roman Empire, and 150 years after paganism was banned, the worship of Isis continued at her temple on the island of Philae in the Nile.

Isis-worship continued until AD 543 at this temple at Philae, Egypt.

Finally, in AD 543 the Emperor Justinian closed her temple, imprisoned her priests and carried off her statues. Ten years later her temple was turned into a church, as commemorated by a contemporary inscription in Greek: 'This good work was done by the well-beloved of God, the Abbot-Bishop Theodore. The Cross has conquered and will ever conquer'.

The longevity of the worship of Isis had much to do with her Mysteries. An experience enclosed within secrecy is powerful and enduring. Herodotus would not even utter the name of Osiris. We know the outer myths but of what was experienced within the Mysteries we are told nothing.

THE SECRET OF THE ELEUSINIAN MYSTERIES

The oldest and most famous of the Mysteries took place at Eleusis in Greece, on the coast of Attica, a twenty-mile journey west from Athens. From Mycenaean to Roman times the Eleusinian Mysteries were the goal of countless pilgrims from all over Greece and far beyond. Anyone, man or woman, free person or slave, could attend the Mysteries provided they spoke Greek and were free of blood-guilt – that is, they had not committed murder. The initiates, called *mystai*, were pledged under penalty of death to a secrecy so faithfully kept that in the course of two thousand years next to nothing of the culminating revelation found its way into record.

Nevertheless, by piecing together clues from allusions to the Mysteries, some sense of what transpired at Eleusis is possible. Certainly the response to the Eleusinian Mysteries was profound. The poet Pindar wrote that 'he who has seen the holy things and goes in death beneath the earth is happy: for he knows life's end and he knows too the new divine beginning', and five hundred years later the historian Plutarch wrote that 'to die is to be initiated'.

Like the Mysteries of Osiris and Isis, of Adonis and Aphrodite, of

Attis and Cybele, the Mysteries at Eleusis had their public face in a well-known myth about life, death and rebirth. Here Persephone was a maiden kidnapped by Hades and taken underground. Her mother Demeter, goddess of agriculture in the Olympian scheme, at once put a curse upon the land, forbidding trees to bear fruit or crops to grow, thereby threatening to extinguish all mankind. Zeus intervened and commanded Hades to return Persephone to the upper world. But she had eaten a pomegranate beneath the earth; she had tasted the food of the dead, said Hades, and she must stay. A compromise was reached: Persephone would live nine months in the upper world with her mother, and three months underground with Hades as his queen, and so life would flourish, then wither, but would be reborn and flourish again.

A Lesser Eleusinia took place in Athens, on the banks of the Ilissos, in late February and early March. Its celebrants were then accepted as candidates for initiation at the Greater Eleusinia in September. After cleansing themselves in the sea, performing sacrifices, fasting and spiritually purifying themselves, the *mystai* set out from Athens in the midst of a great procession of priestesses and priests, including the hierophant (the chief priest), and those who had already been initiated into the Mysteries. A statue of Dionysus was carried at the head of the procession, followed by priestesses carrying the sacred objects concealed in chests, while ecstatic crowds danced and shouted as they travelled to Eleusis along the Sacred Way. The following day was spent in fasting, broken in the evening when the *mystai* drank a draught of barley water from a holy chalice. The next day and the day after, the *mystai* entered the Telesterion, a high-walled and windowless building within the sanctuary of Demeter, arranged with tiered seating on either side to accommodate as many as three thousand initiates. Here in three stages the Mysteries were performed: the *Dromena*, the things done; the *Legomena*, the things said; and the *Deiknymena*, the things shown.

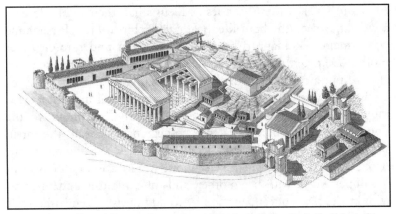

A cut-away site map of the temple complex at Eleusis. In the centre is the Telesterion, a structure that reportedly accommodated up to three thousand initiates.

Initiates came to the revelation after a series of preparations, including fasting, darkness, disorientation and drinking a special potion. Some scholars have said that the barley drink contained a natural psychedelic agent, but most others disagree, saying there is no evidence for that, and anyway all attempts to reproduce the effect have failed. The Mysteries got by for two thousand years most likely on their insights rather than a Mickey Finn.

Several Christian writers who heard something about the Mysteries and felt no compunction about breaking the taboo of secrecy mentioned a ritual that sounds like *ieros gamos*, holy sexual union or sacred marriage. In the second century AD, Clement of Alexandria referred to reports of a bridal chamber and crawling under a bed. Asterius, a fourth-century bishop of Amaseia in Asia Minor, expressed his horror at 'the descent into darkness, the venerated congress of the hierophant with the priestess'. And he went on to ask, 'Are not the torches extinguished and does not the vast and countless assemblage believe that in what is done by the two in the darkness is their salvation?'

Knowing whether this was actually a sexual act is less important than understanding its meaning. At the heart of the various Mysteries was the story of death and life, or rather two types of life, for which the Greeks had two different words, *zoe* and *bio*. Isis, Aphrodite and Demeter possessed *zoe*, eternal life. Osiris and Adonis, and in a sense Persephone too, possessed *bio*; they were creatures of the seasons who lived and died or were taken away to the land of the dead. By means of the sacred marriage, the individual whose life, *bio*, is lived within the rhythms of time was united with *zoe*, the life eternal.

In the case of the Eleusinian Mysteries, Persephone had gone down to the underworld, where she, not her lover Hades, died. It was Demeter who entered into the sacred marriage with Hades, and Persephone was their child. In fact, Persephone was the seasonal aspect of her eternal mother; the daughter is the crop that grows and dies, who is planted like a seed in the underworld to come alive again.

The fundamental experience of these Mysteries, which ritually enacted the initiate's death, may have been that death was an illusion. By submitting himself to death, the initiate was released from the conception of life and death as opposites; he entered into union with

A stone relief from the Telesterion in Eleusis.

THE CONTINUING SIGNIFICANCE OF THE MYSTERIES

The Mysteries, especially the Mysteries at Eleusis, remain fundamental to Freemasonry and esoteric thought to this day. Manly Palmer Hall, who devotes several chapters to the Mysteries in his *Secret Teachings of All Ages*, notes how the influence of the Eleusinian Mysteries spread throughout the world. Albert Pike, the great reformer of the Scottish Rite, draws a direct link between the Telesterion at Eleusis and Freemasons' lodges while explaining the First Degree in his *Morals and Dogma* (see p.64).

The most famous of the ancient religious Mysteries were the Eleusinian, whose rites were celebrated every five years in the city of Eleusis to honor Ceres (Demeter, Rhea, or Isis) and her daughter, Persephone. The initiates of the Eleusinian School were famous throughout Greece for the beauty of their philosophic concepts and the high standards of morality which they demonstrated in their daily lives. Because of their excellence, these Mysteries spread to Rome and Britain, and later the initiations were given in both these countries ...

At the conclusion of this ceremony [the initiate] was hailed as an *Epoptes*, which means one who has beheld or seen directly. For this reason also initiation was termed *autopsy* [from the Greek *autopsia* meaning seeing with one's own eyes].

Manly Palmer Hall, *The Secret Teachings of All Ages*

The Sun is the ancient symbol of the life-giving and generative power of the Deity. To the ancients, light was the cause of life; and God was the source from which all light flowed; the essence of Light, the Invisible Fire, developed as Flame manifested as light and splendour. The Sun was His manifestation and visible image ...

The Moon was the symbol of the passive capacity of nature to produce, the female, of which the life-giving power and energy was the male. It was the symbol of Isis, Astarte, and Artemis, or Diana. The 'Master of Life' was the Supreme Deity, above both ...

The Master of Light and Life, the Sun and the Moon, are symbolized in every Lodge by the Master and Wardens: and this makes it the duty of the Master to dispense light to the Brethren, by himself, and through the Wardens, who are his ministers ...

In the Temple of Eleusis (a sanctuary lighted only by a window in the roof, and representing the Universe), the images of the Sun, Moon, and Mercury, were represented.

Albert Pike, *Morals and Dogma*

the great processes of eternal life, and like all creation, he too became divine. The initiates had forgotten or lost this knowledge, but it was brought back to them by the rituals of the Mysteries.

The secrecy, the sense of brotherhood and the assurance of immortality immensely impressed the Eleusinian Mysteries on the ancient world. The Mysteries are mysterious still. Yet it does seem possible to say that no definite dogma was taught, no doctrinaire interpretation was made of myth or legend. But the things done, the things said and the things shown worked a profound transformation of consciousness that was experienced as a revelation and granted the initiate a direct apprehension of the divine. Like a journey through the Duat of the ancient Egyptians (see p.27), or through the darkness of the Telesterion at Eleusis, Robert Langdon emerges from his journey through the Washington night to see the world in a new way.

PYTHAGORAS AND THE MYSTIC PHILOSOPHERS

If you have come across the phrase 'the music of the spheres' then you already know something about Pythagoras. He was a sixth-century-BC Greek philosopher whose thought combined the spiritual and the rational, and who placed geometry and music at the heart of the workings of the universe. Dan Brown mentions him several times in *The Lost Symbol*. He came from the Mysteries tradition, specifically the Orphic Mysteries, which through the figure of Dionysus had links to the Mysteries of Demeter and Persephone at Eleusis.

Dionysus was the god of the vine and wine and was worshipped by orgiastic rites of drunkeness and dancing which created a sense of liberation from the bounds of man and an intoxicated access to the divine. In one version of the myth, he was the son of Zeus and the ever-useful Persephone (hence the statue of Dionysus carried along

the Sacred Way towards Eleusis at the time of her Mysteries there).
But while still an infant Dionysus was eaten by the evil Titans; Zeus
incinerated them with a thunderbolt and created mankind from
their ashes. Meanwhile Athena had saved Dionysus's heart, which
was implanted in Zeus's thigh, from where Dionysus was reborn,
though another version of the story says Zeus ate the heart and then
re-begot Dionysus by a human mother, Semele. Be that as it may,
mankind is a mixture: the substance of his body comes from the
evil Titans but his soul comes from the divine Dionysus. Only after
a long series of reincarnations and purifications can the soul escape
the cycle of birth and rebirth and be reunited with its divine source.
(Pythagoras himself claimed to have lived four lives that he could
remember in detail and said he had heard the cry of a dead friend
in the bark of a dog.)

The Orphic Mysteries had a reputation for drunkenness and orgies
as well as the crankiness associated with attempts at abstemiousness
and purification. They were looked at askance by the authorities
but they attracted writers, poets, playwrights and philosophers and
would prove to have a lasting influence on Greek thought. 'I am a
child of earth and the starry heaven but my race is of heaven alone',
the Orphic initiates proclaimed.

As Manly Palmer Hall explained in his *Secret Teachings of All Ages*,
'Pythagoras taught that both man and the universe were made in
the image of God; that both being made in the same image, the
understanding of one predicated the knowledge of the other. He
further taught that there was a constant interplay between the
Grand Man (the universe) and man (the little universe). Pythagoras
believed that all the sidereal bodies were alive and that the forms
of the planets and stars were merely bodies encasing souls, minds,
and spirits in the same manner that the visible human form is but
the encasing vehicle for an invisible spiritual organism which is, in
reality, the conscious individual.'

Statue of Pythagoras (1989) by Nikolaos Ikaris, Pythagoreio, Samos island, Greece.
The philosopher, pointing up to the heavens, forms one side of a right-angled triangle.

To Pythagoras we owe our first intimation that the Earth is not the centre of the solar system. He recognized the spherical form of the Earth, and his astronomical researches led to the distinction between real and apparent motions in the movement of the Sun, the planets and the stars. He knew that the Sun only appeared to move round the Earth, but he did not discover the revolution of the Earth on its axis.

Pythagoras sought to explain the world, both spiritual and material, by numbers. He made important observations on the arithmetical proportions that govern musical harmony, and his belief that movements of the heavenly bodies produced concordant notes was later expressed in English as 'the music of the spheres'. His great achievement was the creation of mathematical science.

The influence of Pythagoras was felt on succeeding generations of philosophers, among them Plato and Aristotle who flourished in the fourth century BC. Aristotle quoted him in his *Metaphysics*: 'There is geometry in the humming of the strings. There is music in the spacings of the spheres.' But the influence of Pythagoras was most imprinted on the thoughts of Plato, who shared with him a mystical approach to the soul and its place in the material world, and who accepted from him the idea that mathematics and abstract thinking were a secure basis for philosophical thought and for addressing both science and morals.

Plato believed that men possess immortal souls separate from their mortal bodies. He also believed that knowledge is the recollection of what our souls already know, so that we do not gain knowledge from experience, but rather by using our reasoning capacity to draw more closely to the realm of our souls. For Plato, the true objects of knowledge were not the transient material things of this world, for these he considered to be mere reflections of a higher essence which he called Forms or Ideas. Forms are objects of pure thinking; they are cut off from our experience, but they also motivate us to

FREEMASONRY AND A PYRAMID OF NUMBERS

Freemasonry's preoccupation with numbers, especially three and seven, is well illustrated by Albert Pike's *Morals and Dogma*. In his commentary on the ritual of the Second Degree, for example, Pike writes about the significance of the number ten, how its units can be arranged as a pyramid, and how this all relates to Pythagoras.

> Ten includes all the other numbers. It is especially seven and three; and is called the number of perfection. Pythagoras represented it by the Tetractys, which had many mystic meanings. This symbol is sometimes composed of dots or points, sometimes of commas or yods, and in the Kabalah, of the letters of the name of Deity.

Pike expounds further on the Tetractys in his commentary on the Third Degree:

> The Tetractys thus leads you, not only to the study of the Pythagorean philosophy as to numbers, but also to the Kaballah, and will aid you in discovering the True Word, and understanding what was meant by 'The Music of the Spheres'. Modern science strikingly confirms the ideas of Pythagoras in regard to the properties of numbers, and that they govern in the Universe. Long before his time, nature had extracted her cube-roots and her squares.

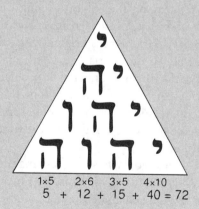

$$1\times5 \quad 2\times6 \quad 3\times5 \quad 4\times10$$
$$5 \; + \; 12 \; + \; 15 \; + \; 40 = 72$$

Hebrew letters arranged in a Tetractys shape, known as a Tetragrammaton.

grasp them, so that the reasoning part of us is drawn to Forms as a kind of mystic communion. This notion of a mystic union with a higher essence would play an important role in later religious and philosophical thought.

PLOTINUS AND NEOPLATONISM

Centuries later, the great Pythagorean themes were still working their effect on the thinking of the Neoplatonic philosophers, men such as Porphyry, born in Tyre in the third century AD. Porphyry wrote a biography of Pythagoras which served as an introduction to Platonic philosophy but in which he was also happy to enlarge on the spiritual and even miraculous side of the Pythagorean tradition, with the intention of providing competition for the Christian gospels.

Porphyry's mentor was Plotinus. Heir to Plato, Aristotle and the Stoics, Plotinus was the last great philosopher of the classical world. He was probably born in Upper Egypt, but we cannot be certain because he was reticent on the subject, saying that the descent of his soul into his body had been a great misfortune, which he did not desire to discuss. Whatever his origins, certainly his culture was Greek, and he came to Alexandria as a youth in the early years of the third century AD to study under the Neoplatonist Ammonius Saccas, a former dockhand who had abandoned the Christian faith, and whose students included the pagan philosopher Longinus and the Christian theologian Origen. These were times when religious thought was still fluid.

Plotinus believed in a god whose highest manifestation he called 'the One'. The One is unity – which is the One. There is nothing more to say. But the One emanates, rather as light streams from the sun or water overflows from a fountain, and its emanations descend through stages until the lowest of realities is reached, the one in which we live. Yet the One is not diminished by this outpouring, rather it embraces all, and in a tremendous arc of emanation and redemption, everything, including our souls, yearns to flow back to the One.

This descent of his soul into corporeal form – this separation from God, this deprivation of union – was why Plotinus was so distressed at being born. But regrettable though it is to inhabit this universe of the senses, we find in it beauty that recalls to our souls the more perfect beauty of the higher realms. 'How lies the path? How come to vision of the inaccessible Beauty?', asks Plotinus, who then teaches how the vision can be obtained: 'This is not a journey for the feet; the feet bring us only from land to land; all this order of things you must set aside and refuse to see; you must close the eyes and call instead upon another vision which is to be waked within you, a vision, the birthright of all, which few can see ... Withdraw into yourself and look ... you are now become very vision; now call up all your confidence, strike forward yet a step – you need a guide no longer – strain and see.' For Plotinus, the gulf between man and God can be crossed by looking within ourselves, because each of us is a microcosm of the universe, each of us is God.

Four times, according to his friend Porphyry, Plotinus saw God. 'Good and kindly, singularly gentle and engaging', Porphyry wrote of Plotinus, 'ever striving towards the divine which he loved with all his being, he laboured strenuously to free himself and rise above the bitter waves of this blood-drenched life: and this is why to Plotinus – God-like and lifting himself often, by the ways of meditation and by the methods Plato teaches in the *Symposium*, to the first and all-transcendent God – that God appeared, the God who has neither shape nor form but sits enthroned above the Intellectual-Principle and all the Intellectual-Sphere.' Indeed, Porphyry himself managed it once: 'To this God, I also declare, I Porphyry, that in my sixty-eighth year I too was once admitted and entered into Union.'

These were nearly the last voices telling of the direct apprehension of the divine before such experiences and views were condemned as heretical by the Christian Church. The Church's other early rival was the organized pagan thought presented as the revelations of Hermes Trismegistus.

HERMES TRISMEGISTUS

Several times in *The Lost Symbol*, Dan Brown mentions Hermetics, Hermes or Hermes Trismegistus. For example, in chapter 9 Robert Langdon reflects on the 'ancient Hermetic adage that proclaimed a belief in the physical connection between heaven and earth. *As above, so below.*' Quite apart from its importance in antiquity, Hermetism would enjoy a renewed and even greater role when it was rediscovered during the Renaissance – and later it would leave its mark on the imagery and ideas of the Illuminati and the Freemasons, as well as on members of the Royal Society, as we will see in the following chapter on the adepts.

The Hermetica was a collection of works that emerged in Egypt in the second and third centuries AD. Since the death of Cleopatra, the last of the Ptolemies, in 30 BC, Egypt had been part of the Roman Empire. Greek culture remained dominant, especially in Alexandria, the city founded by Alexander the Great, and was shared by Greeks and Hellenized Jews and Egyptians, but the old native Egyptian culture was never very far below the surface. Rejecting the complexities of Greek and Egyptian mythology, Hermetism was the intellectualized pagan competition to Christianity. The treatises that make up the Hermetica were almost all written in Greek, but their authorship was shrouded in mystery. Some said they went back centuries, to well before the time of Pythagoras – indeed to the time of Moses – and claimed they were composed by a figure called Hermes Trismegistus, who was also credited with giving laws and letters to

A seventeenth-century copperplate engraving depicting the legendary Hermes Trismegistus.

the Egyptians. The name 'Trismegistus', meaning three-times great, reflected the fact that he was thought to have been a god, a king and a priest. He was a fusion of the Egyptian god Thoth and the Greek Hermes, who had much in common with one another, including their association with the Moon, with medicine and magic, and with the realm of the dead, to which they escorted the souls of the departed – a task which gave them a reputation as oracles.

The writings of the Hermetists fell into two categories. On the technical side were texts on the secrets of plants and stones, and on sympathetic magic, talismans, invocations, astrology and alchemy. The most famous of these writings was *The Emerald Tablet*, which so fascinated Sir Isaac Newton fifteen hundred years later and which he believed contained the secret to discovering the Philosopher's Stone. The other side of the Hermetica were the philosophical and religious texts which were meant to reveal to men the origins, nature and moral properties of the material, human and divine worlds so that they could move towards revelation and salvation.

According to Hermes Trismegistus, everything flowed from a First God, the creator of intellect and souls, and of the material world. Originally formless and inert, the material world was so entirely organized and moulded by the divine that it became a Second God. Mankind, which came from the souls created by the First God, lived within the Second God and had the potential to recognize itself as a Third God. 'I in thee, and thou in me!' is the ecstatic cry in *Poimandres*, one of the Hermetic liturgies. The same is found in the Bible, in the Gospel of St John, 17:21: 'Thou, Father, art in me, and I in thee.' But the meaning is different. Hermetists accepted that all creation, themselves included, was divine. There was no separation. They accused Christians of scorning the world, and they berated the Gnostics for teaching that God was too perfect and good to have created a world so

CONTEXT

AS ABOVE, SO BELOW

The famous phrase 'as above, so below' originated in *The Emerald Tablet*, a brief text ascribed to Hermes Trismegistus. In highly compressed and allusive form, it attempts a comprehensive explanation of the world on its spiritual, intellectual and physical planes. It declares a correspondence between the macrocosm, that is the universe, and the microcosm, that is ourselves. The macrocosm is the microcosm, and vice versa; and so to understand the one is to understand the other. Pythagoras' injunction to know thyself becomes the key to knowing the world. Perhaps borrowing from Plato and Neoplatonists like Plotinus, *The Emerald Tablet* sees creation in terms of a single creative force which brings together opposites, marries the Sun and the Moon, the male and the female, to produce the One. In the Renaissance it was also understood as an alchemical recipe, not least by Sir Isaac Newton who saw in its images of ascension and descent suggestions of various laboratory processes such as solution, separation and distillation. He believed these processes held the secrets of refining metals, prolonging life and achieving earthly bliss – in short, that they were the means of producing the fabled Philosopher's Stone.

Below is Sir Isaac Newton's own translation from the Latin of the *Tabula Smaragdina*, that is *The Emerald Tablet*.

It is true without lying, certain and most true. That which is Below is like that which is Above and that which is Above is like that which is Below to do the miracles of the Only Thing. And as all things have been and arose from One by the mediation of One, so all things have their birth from this One Thing by adaptation. The Sun is its father; the Moon its mother; the Wind hath carried it in its belly; the Earth is its nurse. The father of all perfection in the whole world is here. Its force or power is entire if it be converted into Earth. Separate the Earth from the Fire, the subtle from the gross, sweetly with great industry. It ascends from the Earth to the Heavens and again it descends to the Earth and receives the force of things superior and inferior. By this means you shall have the glory of the whole world and thereby all obscurity shall fly from you. Its force is above all force, for it vanquishes every subtle thing and penetrates every solid thing. So was the world created. From this are and do come admirable adaptations, whereof the process is here in this. Hence am I called Hermes Trismegistus, having the three parts of the philosophy of the whole world. That which I have said of the operation of the Sun is accomplished and ended.

filled with evil and imperfection. Hermetists knew that their souls and reason were derived from the divine and that initiation could return them to the divine. They underwent personal instruction in wisdom and right living, and they engaged in ascetic self-discipline and meditation, the better to turn outwards and embrace the natural beauty of the world, and to turn inwards to contemplate their souls and know themselves. Eventually they would obtain a vision of divine light, and they would be reborn to become one with God and all creation.

About a hundred years later, in AD 313, the Emperor Constantine's Edict of Toleration legalized the practice of Christianity throughout the Roman Empire, and in 391 all expressions of paganism were banned. But even following the complete triumph of Christianity, the argument with its defeated pagan rivals continued. No less a figure than St Augustine, while writing his *City of God* in the early fifth century, thought it important to take issue with Hermes Trismegistus, accusing him of 'god-making', denouncing his gods as 'demons', and charging him with 'futile delusions' and 'pernicious beliefs'. Having completed *The City of God* 'by God's help', Augustine ended his book by asking his readers not to thank him but to 'join with me in rendering thanks to God'. Europe entered the Dark Ages and Hermes Trismegistus slipped into oblivion for a thousand years.

DAN BROWN AND THE ANCIENT MYSTERIES

In *The Lost Symbol*, Dan Brown writes sympathetically about the Mysteries, about Pythagoras and the mystic tradition in philosophy, and about Hermes Trismegistus, all of which promise their followers a direct line to the divine, even an identity with the divine – 'Know ye not that ye are gods?' Even in today's secular climate, their message meets with a ready response from those who take an organic view of the world, who see a strong internal coherence in the universe. Take the popular interest in the butterfly effect, in which a small brief action somewhere can result in a long-term global reaction. Or the Gaia hypothesis which sees our world as a single organism and proposes that the Earth, its seas and its atmosphere are closely integrated to form an interacting system. In *The Lost Symbol* Dan Brown himself mentions the entanglement theory of physics which states that no one object can adequately be described without full mention of other objects, even if each individual object is separated from the others spatially. It all begins to look a lot like the teachings of Hermes Trismegistus, which posited an intimate relationship between the spiritual and material elements of the universe. Everything connects.

But what also appeals to Dan Brown about the philosophies and beliefs of the ancient world is their diversity and their tolerance of one another. It was a quality shared by early Christianity. Before the last half of the third century AD there was no dominant strain of Christianity, no overweening orthodoxy that could accuse others of heresy. Just as Plotinus had studied alongside Origen, an early father of the Church, and both were students of Ammonius Saccas who had himself converted from Christianity to paganism, so the majority of Christians held a variety of beliefs – and yes, some would have had no quarrel with Dan Brown's version of Christianity as set out in *The Da Vinci Code*.

But with the growing power of orthodoxy, Christianity hardened and transformed. Once it was tolerated by the state early in the fourth century and then made the state religion towards the century's end, domination not only by Christianity over paganism but also by one Christian group over the others became a realizable ambition. Varieties of belief were replaced by doctrine and dogma, and the idea of heresy was invented, a thought-crime that could be punishable by death. In *The Lost Symbol*, Dan Brown's emphasis on mysteries and adepts is a more subtle attack on Christianity than that in *The Da Vinci Code*, but it is an attack nonetheless. And more than that, for Dan Brown has used *The Lost Symbol* to broaden his attack on what he sees as the narrow and restrictive dogmas not only of religion but of history and science too, something we will examine in the following chapters on the adepts, the founding fathers and the science of *The Lost Symbol*.

The Adepts

PRACTITIONERS OF LIGHT

'Masonry, like all the Religions, all the Mysteries, Hermeticism and Alchemy, conceals its secrets from all except the Adepts and Sages, or the Elect, and uses false explanations and misinterpretations of its symbols to mislead those who deserve only to be misled; to conceal the Truth, which it calls Light, from them, and to draw them away from it. Truth is not for those who are unworthy or unable to receive it, or would pervert it. So God Himself incapacitates many men, by colour-blindness, to distinguish colours, and leads the masses away from the highest Truth, giving them the power to attain only so much of it as it is profitable to them to know. Every age has had a religion suited to its capacity.'

ALBERT PIKE, *MORALS AND DOGMA*,
FROM HIS COMMENTARY ON THE THIRD DEGREE

Albrecht Dürer

Painter and printmaker Albrecht Dürer, who lived from 1471 to 1528, not only was *the* artist of the German Renaissance but is widely regarded as the greatest German artist of all time. In chapter 68 of *The Lost Symbol*, Robert Langdon describes Dürer as 'the ultimate Renaissance mind – artist, philosopher, alchemist, *and* a lifelong student of the Ancient Mysteries'. Katherine Solomon adds that 'Dürer practiced something called Mystic Christianity – a fusion of early Christianity, alchemy, astrology, and science'. Several of Dürer's works are mentioned in passing in *The Lost Symbol*, but his engraving *Melencolia I* is singled out, with Langdon telling Katherine that in alchemical terms it represents man's continuing failure to turn base metal into gold, while symbolically it represents 'mankind's failed attempt to transform *human* intellect into *god*like power'.

This is not exactly a leisurely exchange. Even as they are telling one another about Dürer, Langdon and Katherine are being hunted by the CIA and are racing through the basement of the Adams Building, part of the Library of Congress. But *Melencolia I* carries a vital clue, and the engraving itself is on display at the nearby National Gallery of Art. However, before Langdon can suggest that it might be worth a look, Katherine says, 'Forget it, Robert, I know what happens when you go into museums' – a wry allusion to the role played by the paintings of Leonardo in *The Da Vinci Code*. Which may be just as well, as *Melencolia I*, says Langdon, is so complex that it 'makes Leonardo da Vinci look overt'. What really interests Langdon is the magic square incorporated into the engraving (see box opposite). This was the very first time that a magic square had appeared in European art, Langdon says excitedly in chapter 70, adding that according to some historians this was Dürer's coded way of indicating that the Ancient Mysteries were now in the possession of European secret societies. Most immediately, the magic square will help Langdon to decipher that Masonic pyramid he carries around in his shoulder bag.

ALBRECHT DÜRER: INFLUENCES FROM ABOVE

In 1512, two years before creating *Melencolia I*, but with the ideas behind it already burgeoning in his mind, Dürer wrote:

> The art of painting is hard to acquire. Therefore, who does not find himself gifted therefore should not undertake it, for it will come from influences from above [the German here is *öbere Eingeissungen*, meaning the influence of the stars, according to common usage]. This great art of painting has been held in high esteem by the mighty kings many hundred years ago. They made the outstanding artists rich and treated them with distinction because they felt that the great masters had an equality with God, as it is written. For, a good painter is inwardly full of figures, and if it were possible for him to live on forever he would always have to pour forth something new from the inner ideas of which Plato writes.

So was Dürer an alchemist, a mystic, an adept of the Ancient Mysteries? And does *Melencolia I* tell us anything about mankind's attempt to acquire godlike powers? For that matter, did Dürer ever think he was a god?

MAGIC SQUARES

Magic squares had been known about – and invested with mystical significance – for many hundreds of years before they found their way to Europe. In particular, mathematicians in China, India and Arabia had been fascinated by their properties.

A magic square is a grid of numbers in which the digits in each row, column and diagonal always add up to the same number (the 'magic constant'). Magic squares can be constructed in grids of any size from 3x3 upwards. For each size of grid, the constant is fixed: for a 3x3 grid, it is 15, for a 4x4 grid it is 34, and so on. For a 3x3 grid, there is only one possible arrangement of the numbers, though this can be rotated or reflected to produce variants. For a 4x4 grid, there are 880 possible arrangements.

In Dürer's 4x4 magic square, not only do the rows, columns and diagonals sum to 34, but so do the 2x2 squares in each of the four corners and the 2x2 square at the centre of the grid:

16	3	2	13
5	10	11	8
9	6	7	12
4	15	14	1

The middle two numbers on the bottom row – 15 and 14 – reflect the date the engraving was produced, and the numbers to either side of them represent the artist's initials: 4 is D for Dürer, and 1 is A for Albrecht.

Albrecht Dürer was born in Nuremberg, the first son and the third of eighteen children of a less-than-prosperous goldsmith from Ajtas in Hungary. Ajtas is linked to the Hungarian word for door, which translates into German as *tür* or *dür*. When later Dürer obtained a coat of arms, he used a door as its central device. Some might see something suggestive of alchemy in the father's work with metals and even in his name and Dürer's later choice of the door device. And they might be right. Though the philosophical side of Hermetism was rediscovered in Renaissance Italy, the technical strand of the Hermetica, which dealt with things such as alchemy, had much earlier made its way north of the Alps by a separate route. It is entirely possible that Dürer was raised in an environment where certain people were familiar with aspects of the Hermetica, although there is no evidence that he was.

At first, Dürer was apprenticed to his father, from whom he learnt to use the tools and materials of the goldsmith's craft. This would prove invaluable in his future artistic career, in which engraving played a major part. There is very little difference between engraving a design on a precious locket or box made of gold and engraving an image on copper plate, except that you can multiply the latter by printing. In fact, the greatest engravers of the fifteenth century were not originally painters or book illuminators but goldsmiths who applied their age-old technique to the new process of printing. But this had not been done before in Nuremberg; Dürer would be the first.

By the age of fifteen Dürer was realizing his artistic powers, which extended well beyond the often mechanical work of goldsmithing, and with his father's blessing he was apprenticed to the workshop of Michael Wolgemut, a leading Nuremberg painter. There Dürer learnt to work with pen and brush, to draw from life, and to use watercolours, gouache and oils. Wolgemut also produced woodcuts for commercial books, introducing Dürer to the graphic medium that would eventually disseminate his work throughout Europe.

In the tradition of young artists at the time, at the age of eighteen Dürer was sent away to broaden his experience by working under a series of different masters. He travelled to Holland, to Alsace and to Basel in Switzerland, which was then the foremost book production centre in Europe. Marriage was a requirement for setting up on his own as an independent master, and so in 1494, at the age of 23, Dürer returned to Nuremberg where he married, apparently by arrangement, a young woman called Agnes Frey. In the event, it turned out to be a childless and unhappy relationship, with Dürer's friends accusing Agnes of making him miserable with her shrewishness, her greed and her pious nastiness. Probably Agnes thought that she had married a painter in the medieval tradition, much like a tailor who produced to order; instead her husband was discovering in himself a divine gift and needed to nourish his mind on the humanities and mathematics. Quite simply, he outgrew her intellectually, and Agnes reacted bitterly to his neglect.

Dürer would go off to libraries, studios and clubs and spend his time talking over his ideas with a circle of friends that included artists, scientists and scholars, bishops, patricians and noblemen. His closest friend was Willibald Pirckheimer, whose family was one of the richest and oldest in Nuremberg. Pirckheimer studied at the universities of Pavia and Padua in northern Italy, which were steeped in humanist traditions, and he initiated Dürer into the Greek and Roman classics and kept him informed of the latest developments in philosophy. He would also suggest cryptic subjects for Dürer's prints.

DÜRER AND THE ITALIAN RENAISSANCE

In 1494, almost immediately after his marriage, Dürer travelled alone to Venice and possibly elsewhere in northern Italy, remaining there for half a year. This sojourn in the south – in the land where classical antiquity had been reborn – had a marked effect on Dürer's style, and it also marked the beginning of the Renaissance in the countries north of the Alps. The Italians, he said, had brought about a 'regrowth' in the arts after they had been 'hiding for a millennium', and he felt that Germans should participate too. For the next ten years, his creative output was prodigious.

Throughout his life, Dürer's work was marked by two radically different qualities, one the patient observation of detail, the other a visionary quality. Even in his beautifully realized gouache-and-watercolour painting *The Hare*, the detail is at once obsessively objective and startlingly hyper-real. Dürer spoke of himself as being full of 'inward figures', and it is as though these figures insisted on infusing even his nature observations with their spirits.

In 1505 Dürer went again to Italy, where he was in contact with Leonardo Da Vinci, travelled to Bologna to receive instruction in what he called the 'secret art of perspective', and lived in Venice with the elderly Giovanni Bellini. Bellini's sensuous and richly coloured paintings had done much to transform Italian art, and Dürer said he was still the best painter in the city. Bellini reciprocated the esteem. This time Dürer stayed away a year and a half, returning to Nuremberg in 1507. Back home, he began writing his treatises on geometry and proportion in art, and entered into a long and brilliant period in which he produced many of his greatest masterpieces, among them the painting of *Adam and Eve,* the *Rhinoceros* woodcut, and the engravings of *The Knight, Death and the Devil*, of *St Jerome in his Study* and of *Melencolia I.*

MELANCHOLY AND THE CREATIVE SPIRIT

Dürer engraved *The Knight, Death and the Devil* in 1513, and *St Jerome in his Study* and *Melencolia I* the following year. They bear no compositional relation to one another and cannot be considered as companion pieces, but each addresses a theme – the first moral, the

Albrecht Dürer's *Melencolia I*.

second theological, the third intellectual – and together they form a spiritual unity. *The Knight* represents the Christian in the practical world of decision and action; *St Jerome* is the life of sacred contemplation; and *Melencolia I* depicts the secular genius in the worlds of science and art. The first two make their statements clearly. But *Melencolia I* presents an enigma, not to mention a sense of disorder. Meanwhile, though we will get back to it later (see p.117), it is relevant to know that in the diary he kept while working on *The Knight*, Dürer mentions a rumour that Martin Luther has been assassinated and writes 'O God, if Luther is dead, who shall henceforth so clearly expound to us the Holy Gospels?' Luther was excommunicated by Pope Leo X in 1521, but when Dürer was creating these etchings both he and Luther were still Roman Catholics.

The Oxford English Dictionary gives a long history of the definitions of the word 'melancholy'. One current definition is 'sadness and depression of spirits', but in Dürer's time melancholy was not a mood that would come and go; rather, it was one of the four humours, those fundamental qualities of the human constitution. Blood was moist and warm, and was associated with spring and youth; phlegm was moist and cold, and was associated with winter, night and old age; choler was hot and dry, and was associated with summer and manly maturity; while melancholy, dry and cold, was associated with the earth, with autumn, evening and entering into one's sixties. Everyone possessed all four humours, and in a healthy person they were reasonably balanced, though one of the four would almost certainly dominate, so that a person could be described as sanguine (blood), choleric, phlegmatic or melancholic.

However, in place of this notion of the humours Dürer has substituted thoughts collected during his Italian travels and his encounters with Renaissance philosophy. To the traditional medieval view of the melancholic were opposed the words of Aristotle who said 'All truly outstanding men, whether distinguished in philosophy, in statecraft, in poetry or in the arts, are melancholics'. Moreover, the connection made in the Middle Ages between the humours and the planets – with Venus as phlegmatic, Mars as choleric, Jupiter as sanguine and Saturn as melancholic – was now used to give a further boost to the quality of melancholy, for the Florentines, who had rediscovered Plotinus, found that he exalted Saturn far above the other planets. Jupiter symbolized the soul, but Saturn symbolized the mind, and the mind was at a higher level than the soul. Thanks to Aristotle and Plotinus, the northern Italian Renaissance placed the halo of the sublime on Saturn and on melancholy, and the most illustrious members of the Florentine Renaissance, not least Lorenzo de Medici, 'the Magnificent', were quick to declare themselves 'Saturnians'.

In the popular mind, however, Saturn remained a malignant planet, and its baleful effects needed to be warded off by talismans. Sanguine Jupiter was called upon, which explains the presence of the magic square in Dürer's *Melencolia I*. The sixteen-cell magic square was known as the *Mensula Jovis*, the Table of Jupiter, and regardless of its mathematical properties it had the simple talismanic effect of turning evil into good and dispelling all worries and fears – of counteracting any supposed negative influence of Saturn.

THE SPIRITUAL TRAGEDY OF *MELENCOLIA I*

Dürer took this material and worked it into the expression of a spiritual tragedy. The figure of Melancholy, winged yet flightless, equipped with the tools of art and science yet sitting in brooding idleness, represents creation reduced to despair. 'Melencolia' was the spelling at the time. But why the number one? The engraving is not the first of a series, and Dürer never intended that there should be others. The number one refers to this one image and is part of the description.

The literary source for this image was *De Occulta Philosophia* by Cornelius Agrippa of Nettesheim. Published in 1509, it was dedicated to a friend of Willibald Pirckheimer's and so is likely to have found its way into Dürer's hands pretty quickly. The book sets out Plotinus's idea of a great fountain or stream of light pouring forth from the One, embracing all, and then returning to the One. Man participates in this flowing and can receive direct 'inspiration from above' (that same phrase Dürer used, meaning the influence of the stars). Agrippa distinguishes three kinds of genius, each of whom acts under the impulse of Saturn. The first has an imagination that is stronger than the mind or reason. He will turn out to be a wonderful artist, craftsman or architect. In the second, reason predominates; he will become a scientist, physician or statesman. The third is the person in whom the intuitive mind outweighs the other faculties; this person will come to know the secrets of the divine. In this system, Dürer's Melencolia can be classed as the first, as number one. This is the least exalted form. The figure can think, build and invent, but her imagination cannot go beyond her mind or reason, which is restricted; she has no access to the metaphysical world.

Melencolia I is in fact Dürer's spiritual portrait of himself. He is aware of inspirations from above but he cannot command them to his will or enter into their sphere and so feels powerless and dejected. Dürer had been studying mathematics, geometry, proportion and perspective with the aim of finding the formula for absolute beauty, only finally to confess 'But what absolute beauty is, I know not. Nobody knows it except God'. And then came Dürer's complete retreat from any special communion with the divine: 'The lie is in our understanding, and darkness is so firmly entrenched in our mind that even our groping will fail.'

DÜRER AND MARTIN LUTHER

Five years after *Melencolia I*, Dürer's spiritual crisis came to a head. 'Dürer is in bad shape', said his friend Pirckheimer. A year later, in 1520, Dürer told another friend 'If God helps me to see Martin Luther, I will diligently make his portrait and engrave it as a lasting memory of the Christian man who has helped me out of great anxieties'. When Luther was excommunicated the following year, Dürer was already his follower. Nor was he alone; in 1525 the city of Nuremberg officially decided to reject papal authority. Soon all of Northern Europe had followed suit.

By the time of his death in 1528 Dürer was no longer ascribing his special talents to 'influences from above' – the stars – as he had done back in 1512. In his last writings, he claimed simply that he was born with them. Nor did he any longer liken the artist to God; the artist is merely credited with 'power given by God'. Plotinus had written of Phidias's statue of Zeus, one of the Seven Wonders of the World, that it had not been formed from anything visible, 'but in such a way as Zeus himself would appear were he to show himself to human eyes'. The thinkers of the Italian Renaissance borrowed from the Neoplatonists to establish their humanistic and mankind-centred view of the world, but that humanism led to that massive rejection of the Church known as the Protestant Reformation, and that too had its own orthodoxies. Plotinus was speaking blasphemy when he described Phidias's work in such a way. Doubtful about what God would think of images, Dürer came close to giving up his work as painter, woodcutter and engraver altogether. His friend Pirckheimer, who had supported Luther's reforms at the beginning, later became disgusted by the whole business. 'Things have come to a pass that the Popish scoundrels are made to appear virtuous by the Evangelical ones. The old crowd has cheated us with hypocrisy and trickery; the new one proposes to do shameful and criminal things in the open.' But Dürer never wavered in his support for Luther, and when he died, said his close friend Pirckheimer, he died 'a good Lutheran'.

Mal'akh: The Evil Adept

'Mal'akh had learned long ago that through proper application of the Art, a practitioner could open a portal to the spiritual realm. The invisible forces that existed there, much like man himself, came in many forms, both good and evil.'

The Lost Symbol [CHAPTER 96]

Mal'akh is the incarnation of prejudice, superstition, the irrational – of all those things opposed to the furtherance of knowledge. He is the Dark against the Light. As Mal'akh himself explains in chapter 77, he was led into the world of the occult when he discovered the writings of Aleister Crowley, 'a visionary mystic from the early 1900s – whom the church had deemed "the most evil man who ever lived." *Great minds are always feared by lesser minds.*' In fact it was not the Church that tagged Crowley as evil, it was the popular press in England: 'the wickedest man in the world', they said in a series of exposées in 1921 which gave Crowley the notoriety he craved. He gave himself the titles of 'the great Beast' and 'the Beast 666'.

Aleister Crowley (1875–1947) became interested in magic while an undergraduate at Cambridge and was soon a member of the Hermetic Order of the Golden Dawn, founded in Britain by three Freemasons, which aimed at spiritual development and practised theurgy, that is rituals aimed at achieving union with the divine. The Irish poet William Butler Yeats was also a member. But Crowley was expelled for extreme practices, leading him to settle at Cefalu in Sicily where he established his own religion, Thelema, which, he declared, had superseded Christianity. Thelema is from the Greek meaning 'I want, I wish, I desire'. The essence of his creed, as set out in his 1909 *Book of the Law*, was 'Do what thou wilt shall be the whole of the Law', a maxim which never left him short of disciples, especially young women. 'And I rave; and I rape and rip and I rend' is a line from his poem *Hymn to Pan*. The 1921 London newspaper campaign against Crowley included rumours of drugs, orgies and magical ceremonies involving the sacrifice of babies (though there is no evidence of the last), which culminated in his expulsion from Italy in 1923. This came as something of a shock, as Crowley was convinced that he could control reality by magical thinking. He spent the rest of his life in London, much of it in the Fitzroy Tavern in Charlotte Street, Bloomsbury, where he became well known, in

the words of the publican, as 'a megolomaniac with a talent for self-dramatisation'. Though Crowley sounds very much the model for Mal'akh, he did not go so far as to offer *himself* as a blood sacrifice, as Brown's character does.

Having first read Aleister Crowley, Mal'akh, or Andros Dareios as he still called himself, looked into the *Key of Solomon*, in Latin the *Clavis Salomonis*, a grimoire or book of magic attributed to King Solomon, known since the Italian

Aleister Crowley: maverick magus at his altar.

Renaissance. Possibly it was inspired by earlier material such as the Kabbalah and the Hermetica, but nothing of its content has been demonstrated to date earlier than the fourteenth century. The *Key of Solomon* tells of rituals, charms, sacrifices and incantations that can be used to control reality, to exercise one's will.

When a crow flies into his open window and cannot escape, Andros recognizes this as a sign. '*I am being urged onward.* Clutching the bird in one hand, he stood at the makeshift altar in his kitchen and raised a sharp knife, speaking aloud the incantation he had memorized. "Camiach, Eomiahe, Emial, Macbal, Emoii, Zazean … by the most holy names of the angels in the Book of Assamaian, I conjure thee that thous assist me in this operation by the power of the One True God."' The words are straight out of the *Key of Solomon*, but instead of Mal'akh's crow it recommends a bat.

The ritualism continues when Mal'akh draws blood from Katherine Solomon's arm, just as he has already drawn blood from the arm of her brother Peter Solomon. Mal'akh's aim is nothing less than to become divine.

Solomon: Mystic and Magician

In *The Lost Symbol* Mal'akh begins life as Zachary Solomon, the son of Peter Solomon, and both characters can be seen as referring back to the original King Solomon. Peter is the Solomon of wisdom, head of the Smithsonian Institution, also head of the Supreme Council Thirty-third Degree of the Scottish Rite of Freemasons. But Zachary, who turned his back on wisdom and responsibility, resorts to the occult magic of *The Key of Solomon* to advance his evil intentions. *The Key of Solomon* itself emerged from a long post-biblical tradition found in legends, fables, rabbinical stories and the Koran, which portray Solomon as a figure possessing magical and mystical powers.

The Bible accounts of King Solomon's wisdom (for example 1 Kings 3 & 4) spread his reputation far and wide and throughout all ages. Soon he was also famed as a mystic and a magician. In Islam, as in the Old Testament, Solomon is the paragon of wisdom; he is the author of the saying that 'the beginning of wisdom is the fear of God', and he is also accounted wise for his knowledge of the unseen. As Suleiman and as a Muslim he is portrayed in the Koran as being in communion with the natural world and speaking 'the language of the birds' (Koran 27:17). God has also given him dominion over the spirit world: 'We subjected the wind to him, so that it blew softly at his bidding wherever he directed it; and the devils, too, among whom were builders and divers and others bound with chains' (Koran 38:35-36). Among those builders were the jinn, the supernatural beings of Muslim legend that can take human or animal form, whom Solomon commanded to build the Temple for him.

Solomon is also the epitome of the mystical love of women as in the Song of Solomon in the Old Testament. In Islam this mystical love is expressed in the story of Belkis, the Queen of Sheba, who was converted from paganism by Solomon who taught her the difference between illusion and the One Reality as expressed in the *shahadah*, 'there is no God but God', and thus became his consort. The Queen of Sheba was the expression of cosmic infinitude which complemented Solomon who was the expression of wisdom or self.

In both the Jewish and the Islamic worlds, Solomon is traditionally associated with stories of the marvellous. He became the subject of rabbinic and kabbalistic lore in which he is portrayed as a fabulous figure, a master magician possessing occult powers. In one kabbalistic legend Solomon orders a demon to convey Hiram, the King of Tyre, down to the seven compartments of hell so that on his return he can reveal to Solomon all he has seen in the underworld.

THE SEAL OF SOLOMON

The Seal of Solomon, the device adorning his seal-ring, is said to have come down to Solomon from heaven. The design consisted of two interlaced or intersecting triangles, one pointing up, the other down, and these were placed within two concentric circles between which was engraved the words 'the most greatest name of God'. In alchemy the upward- and downward-pointing triangles represent fire and water, and they symbolize the combination of opposites and hence transmutation. There are some who see a sexual symbolism in these triangles, and indeed in Egyptian hieroglyphs the V-shape does seem to be taken from the shape of the female pubis, while if the upward-pointing triangle is taken to be a phallus, then the fusion of the two can symbolize harmony in the universe and between the sexes. Be that as it may, the device has been a frequent motif used on coins in the Islamic world and as a decoration. Also known as the Star of David, it is the six-pointed star on the flag of the modern state of Israel, and it appears on every dollar bill among the pattern of stars on the obverse of the Great Seal of the United States.

Solomon also appears in *The Thousand and One Nights*, where in the *Tale of the Fisherman and the Jinn* he has used his seal-ring to imprison an evil spirit in a jar for 1800 years.

Sir Isaac Newton

For those in search of secret knowledge, Sir Isaac Newton has always shown the way. That at any rate is what Dan Brown has Robert Langdon thinking to himself in chapter 85 of *The Lost Symbol*. Yet it is not a notion that crossed the mind of Manly Palmer Hall, author of *The Secret Teachings of All Ages*, which by Dan Brown's own admission is one of his major sources of esoteric knowledge: Hall has nothing to say about Newton in his book. But *The Secret Teachings* was published in 1928, and the remarkable secret life of Isaac Newton was only discovered eight years later. The mysteries are still being unravelled to this day.

THE POWERS OF REASON

First there is the orthodox story about Isaac Newton, the familiar tale you would have heard until 1936 when his papers on alchemy began to become public after being held for centuries in a private collection. Newton was born in Lincolnshire in 1642, he was an undergraduate at Cambridge, but his studies there were interrupted when the university was closed down during the outbreak of the Great Plague in 1664. Sometime during the next two years, while he was sitting in his garden, the famous apple fell, the one that may or may not have bounced off his head but which certainly set him thinking and led to his formulation of the law of gravitation – which he formally expounded in 1684. Newton showed that the force of gravity between two bodies, for example the Sun and the Earth, or for that matter his head and an apple, is in direct proportion to the product of the masses of the bodies and inversely proportional to the square of the distance between them.

He described the law of gravitation more completely in his great work *Principia Mathematica*, published in 1687, where he also set out his three laws of motion. The first states that 'every body persists in its state of being at rest or of moving uniformly straight forward, except insofar as it is compelled to change its state by force impressed'; the second mathematically defines the relationship between acceleration, force and mass; and the third states that 'to every action there is always an equal and opposite reaction: or the forces of two bodies on each other are always equal and are directed in opposite directions'. Newton also conducted experiments in optics and the nature of light. All this was well known and established Newton as one of the greatest scientists of all time, and a champion for the argument that the mysteries of the universe can be laid bare by the powers of reason. Yet this was the same Newton, as we have seen (p.102), who translated *The Emerald Tablet* of Hermes Trismegestus and used it as the basis for alchemical experiments, believing that it was the key to the Philosopher's Stone. But of his interest in the occult nothing was known, or at least nothing was much revealed.

NEWTON, FREEMASONS AND SOLOMON'S TEMPLE

Something of Isaac Newton's writings on religion were known, however. He wrote four hundred and seventy books in all, many of them on theological subjects and several about the Temple of Solomon. Newton was convinced that Solomon was the greatest philosopher of all time, and he also believed that he owed his own breakthrough formulation of the law of gravity to his close reading of those portions of the Bible, 1 Kings and 2 Chronicles, which give in great detail the measurements of Solomon's Temple. God would not have

Portrait of Isaac Newton (James McArdell, 1760).

had the measurements set down in the Bible if they were not significant, and so Newton bent himself to discover their code. Among other things, Newton saw in those figures all manner of prophecies of great and terrible events that would take place over the coming four hundred years, including the Second Coming of Christ in 1948 and the end of the world in 2060.

The Temple of Solomon was of course of central interest to Freemasons too. Newton, who died in 1727, a decade after the founding of the Grand Lodge, was never himself a Mason, but Freemasonry did attract eminent intellectuals, including several members of the Royal Society, of which Newton became president in 1703. And John Theophilus Désaguliers, the experimental philosopher and follower of Newton, became Grand Master of the United Lodge in 1719. Newton would have had no difficulty in sharing an interest in the mysteries of Solomon's Temple with the Freemasons. In fact scholars have argued that in Newton's fascination for the mysterious proportions of the Temple of Solomon one is encountering the milieu that gave rise to early Freemasonry. Newton represented the tensions of the time: the mix of competing religious and scientific positions. It may well be, goes the argument, that Freemasonry was an innovation that fostered intellectual discussion while neutralizing doctrinal conflict by its new form of ritual to worship the Grand Architect of the Universe. The origins of Freemasonry can be seen as lying not only in the medieval English and Scottish stonemasons' guilds and in the dawn of the Enlightenment, but also in occult readings of the Bible and in the corpus of Hermes Trismegistus.

STANDING ON THE SHOULDERS OF GIANTS

When the Hermetica appeared in Western Europe at the beginning of the Italian Renaissance it was found acceptable by many Christians because of its extreme antiquity. Here were the writings of the ancient Egyptian priest Hermes Trismegistus, a man who was supposed to have lived at least as far back as the days of Moses, whose ideas seemed to encompass and therefore prophesy Greek philosophy from Pythagoras to Plotinus and to anticipate Christianity too. But in 1614 when scholarship proved that the Hermetica was composed only in the second and third centuries AD, that is after the rise of Neoplatonism and of early Christianity, it was discredited in Christian circles where its influence quickly waned.

But that applied only to the philosophical strain of Hermetism; the technical and largely alchemical form persisted and has been influential in the West where magic, occultism, alchemy, unorthodox mysticism and an interest in Ancient Egypt have remained strong. Newton himself was heir to the alchemical writings of Hermes Trismegistus, whom he supposed to be a real person. Irrational as the Hermetic tradition might seem, there is a good historical argument that the pursuit of alchemy laid the foundations for modern chemistry. When Newton made his famous remark, 'If I have seen further it is only by standing on the shoulders of giants', he was thinking back to the Ancient Mysteries.

NEWTON AND THE DIVINE

In chapter 85 of *The Lost Symbol*, when Langdon and Katherine find sanctuary at Washington's National Cathedral, they talk with its dean, who is also a Freemason, about the clues they have found thanks to Dürer's magic square. Jeovus Sanctus Unus reads the decrypt, the One True God. It is an anagram, says the dean, who ought to know about such things, as his own name is Colin Galloway, an anagram for 'a wooly calling'. Jeova Sanctus Unus, he explains, can be reworked as Isaacus Neuutonus, where the Latin I and J are interchangeable as are the Latin U and V. Isaac Newton wrote his name that way, says Dean Galloway, because like the adepts of the ancient past he understood that he was divine. Newton rejected the Trinity and the divinity of Jesus; the worship of Jesus was blasphemous idolatry, he believed. Such beliefs could put Newton in that long line of heresies that has included Arians, Gnostics and Cathars. When Dan Brown, or his mouthpiece Colin Galloway, says that Newton knew himself to be divine, he may have been thinking of the Gnostic and Cathar belief that a piece of God is within us all, an idea held by Plotinus too, but the impression one gets of Newton's beliefs is that he was content to be the tool of the divine, not the divine itself. Though Newton had been born into a conventional Anglican family, he was more like the Deists, for he saw the pattern of the divine in creation but otherwise rejected the idea of God's intervention in the world. On his deathbed he refused to take the sacrament since it was meant to provide divine grace and forgiveness, a notion Newton dismissed as nonsense.

THE LAST MAGICIAN

'About 6 weeks at spring, and 6 at the fall, the fire in the elaboratory scarcely went out, which was well furnished with chemical materials as bodies, receivers, heads, crucibles, etc, which was made very little use of, the crucibles excepted, in which he fused his metals; he would sometimes, tho' very seldom, look into an old mouldy book which lay in his elaboratory, I think it was titled *Agricola de Metallis*, the transmuting of metals being his chief design … His brick furnaces, *pro re nata*, he made and altered himself without troubling a bricklayer.' So wrote Newton's assistant in 1728, the year after his master's death. The man now famous as one of the greatest scientists in the areas of light and optics, the motions of the planets, and mathematics and physics, was also an alchemist. The *Principia Mathematica* represented only a small proportion of his efforts, most of which were directed to writing about theology, the history of the Church, the chronology of ancient kingdoms, and about prophecy and alchemy. Newton's alchemical writings amount to more than a million words in manuscript. As his assistant observed, 'He very rarely went to bed until two or three of the clock, sometimes not till five or six, lying about four or five hours, especially at springtime or autumn, at which time he used to employ about six weeks in his laboratory, the fire scarce going out night or day. What his aim might be I was unable to penetrate into'.

After his death the Royal Society deemed that his alchemical researches were 'not fit to be printed', and the papers fell to a private collector, only to be rediscoverd in the twentieth century. Modern scholars now concede that Newton was first and foremost an alchemist, and they also admit that the obvious inspiration for his laws of light and theory of gravity came from his alchemical work.

But of this work, as Dan Brown mentions in chapter 133 of *The*

Lost Symbol, Newton wrote his friend and fellow scientist Robert Boyle that it was necessary to maintain 'high silence' in publicly discussing the principles of alchemy, for it is 'not to be communicated without immense damage to the world if there be any verity in [the warning of the] Hermetic writers. There are other things besides the transmutation of metals which none but they understand'. That Newton never published a work on alchemy cannot be taken to mean that he felt he had failed in what he called this 'Great Work', rather that thought he had gained enough success to think that he might be on the track of something of fundamental importance, and so good reason for keeping 'high silence'.

Long viewed as the high apostle of scientific rationalism, Sir Isaac Newton turns out to be a very different figure in the history of Western thought. For Dan Brown he epitomizes the confluence of reason and mysticism, pragmatism and philosophy, science and alchemy. Newton admires the magnificence of the divine in the ordering of the universe, and perhaps for that very reason he cannot submit to narrow man-made doctrines. For Dan Brown this all harks back to an earlier time when man was excited by the wonder of discovery and was free to explore beyond boundaries. It is the wonder of the child. Brown is suggesting that in choosing between reason on the one hand, faith on the other, we have lost our way, have lost the vital link that exists between the two. Katherine picks up on this when she says that science, which for centuries had derided religion as superstition, is now having to admit that its next big challenge is 'the science of faith and belief ... the power of focused conviction and intention'. She is talking about her own work in noetics. But noetic science was an important discovery for Dan Brown himself, one he made long ago and has kept abreast of ever since, and has now turned into a major theme in *The Lost Symbol* – it is the way forward, he believes.

Manly Palmer Hall

Manly Palmer Hall (1901–90) is most famous for *The Secret Teachings of All Ages*, which according to Dan Brown in a 16 October 2009 television interview 'really is a core book for a lot of what I research and a lot of what I believe'. The subtitle of Hall's magnum opus is *An Encylopedic Outline of Masonic, Hermetic, Qabbalistic and Rosicrucian Symbolical Philosophy*. A mammoth work running to 750 pages in its present edition, it was originally published in 1928 when Hall was only twenty-seven. It immediately established him in esoteric circles.

PHILOSOPHER TO THE STARS

Born in Canada, he was abandoned by both parents and lived a shifting childhood with his grandmother, until an encounter with a fortune teller in Santa Monica when he was eighteen set him on the life-long path of mystic philosopher. In a career spanning more than seventy years, Hall wrote over 200 books and essays, innumerable magazine articles, and delivered over eight thousand lectures in both the United States and abroad. In 1934, Hall founded the Philosophical Research Society in Los Angeles, California; its library, from which the psychoanalyst Carl Jung borrowed volumes he could find nowhere else, contains a vast collection of obscure and scarce items in the areas of consciousness studies, psychology, Eastern and Western religions, mysticism, metaphysics, science and both classical and modern philosophy.

In the Los Angeles of the 1930s to 1950s, Manly Hall was a name to be reckoned with. His friends included movie people such as Bela Lugosi, Gloria Swanson, Sam Goldwyn and Cecil B DeMille, and also the writer Aldous Huxley, author of *Brave New World* and the mescalin classic *The Doors of Perception*. Hall's lectures on the

Hermetics, the Rosicrucians, the Freemasons and almost every other occult and mystical subect drew huge crowds, and his prolific outbook of books reached millions of readers, including president Harry S Truman. Even into the 1970s he was attracting visits from Elvis Presley to the astronaut Edgar Mitchell, founder of the Institute of Noetic Sciences.

LOST MYSTERIES

The cities of the ancient world, Hall wrote in his *Secret Teachings*, had their communities of philosophers and mystics versed in nature's lore, and 'the more important of these groups were known as the Mysteries', among the most celebrated being those of Isis and Eleusis. 'Many of the great minds of antiquity were initiated into these secret fraternities by strange and mysterious rites', and 'much of the ritualism of Freemasonry', Hall continued, 'is based on the trials to which candidates were subjected by the ancient hierophants before the keys of wisdom were entrusted to them.' In their secret theological system 'God was considered as the Grand Man and, conversly, man as the little god. Continuing this analogy, the universe was regarded as a man and, conversly, man as a miniature universe' – macrocosm and microcosm, as above, so below.

As an aid to understanding, the early priests placed a statue of a man in the sanctuary of the temple. 'This human figure symbolized the Divine Power in all its intricate manifestations. ... Then came the age of idolatry. The Mysteries decayed from within. The secrets were lost and none knew the identity of the mysterious man who stood over the altar. It was remembered only that the figure was a sacred and glorious symbol of the Universal Power, and it finally came to be looked upon as a god – the One in whose image man was made.' In time the priests' 'lack of spiritual understanding brought the temple down in ruins about their heads and the statue crumbled with the civilization that had forgotten its meaning'. Manly Hall's purpose in *The Secret Teachings* was to restore that lost knowledge, so that 'the criers of the Mysteries speak again, bidding all men welcome to the House of Light'.

FREEMASONS AND THE MYSTERIES

Hall saw the Freemasons as those criers of the Mysteries, emissaries of a priceless heritage: 'within the Freemasonic Mysteries lie hidden the long-lost arcana sought by all people since the genesis of human reason'. Hall was not yet a Freemason when he wrote *The Secret Teachings* (he was raised as a Mason only in 1954), though it is replete with references to Freemasonry, including a vast chapter in three parts called *The Ancient Mysteries and Secret Societies Which Have Influenced Modern Masonic Symbolism*, and another called *Freemasonic Symbolism*. But these have been criticized by some Freemasons for being written by an uninformed outsider.

Nevertheless, in 1973, forty-five years after he published *The Secret Teachings*, the Supreme Council of the Scottish Rite saw fit to honour Manly Hall by conferring upon him their highest honour, the Thirty-third Degree – though not in Washington, DC's House of the Temple with drinks all round from a human skull, but instead in Los Angeles at Hall's own Philosophical Research Society. The PRS continues to this day and has been augmented since Hall's death by the creation of the University of Philosophical Research, which offers State of California approved Masters of Art degrees in Consciousness Studies and Transformational Psychology.

Manly Palmer Hall. *The Secret Teachings* was published when he was only 27.

MAN AS GOD IN THE BIBLE?

A major theme of *The Lost Symbol* is that men are gods. This can be taken in many ways, both literally and figuratively, and as an injunction that mankind must assume responsibility for itself, for its actions, for our future and for the nature of our world. But in chapter 82 Dan Brown claims that the Bible itself has told men that they are gods. The realisation that man is god was fundamental to the Mysteries and to the Hermetics, he says. And then he adds: 'Even the Holy Bible cried out in Psalms 82:6: *Ye are gods!*' But Dan Brown has taken those words out of context and has misinterpreted what the Bible has to say. All eight verses of Psalms 82 are here given in full.

1 God standeth in the congregation of the mighty; he judgeth among the gods.

2 How long will ye judge unjustly, and accept the persons of the wicked? Selah.

3 Defend the poor and fatherless: do justice to the afflicted and needy.

4 Deliver the poor and needy: rid them out of the hand of the wicked.

5 They know not, neither will they understand; they walk on in darkness: all the foundations of the earth are out of course.

6 I have said, Ye are gods; and all of you are children of the Most High.

7 But ye shall die like men, and fall like one of the princes.

8 Arise, O God, judge the earth: for thou shalt inherit all nations.

In this chapter the judges are encouraged and reproved, and they are reminded that though they may inflate themselves with thoughts of being gods, or like gods, they are merely men. God stands among his people whom he calls gods, or like gods; they are children of on high and have received his word. And his word obliges them to act on behalf of the poor, the afflicted, and so on. But instead the judges have been negligent. And now God says 'Ye are gods', that is the judges are clothed with God's power and authority to dispense justice. They must carry out their duty. That is their task, not to puff themselves up with pride and position, for like any man, like any prince, they too will someday die.

In other words, Psalms 82 is saying man must act responsibly. It is not saying that man is god.

DAN BROWN AND MANLY HALL

Dan Brown has said that *The Secret Teachings of All Ages* is a core book for the researches that have helped form his beliefs. It is certainly a giant compendium of esoteric history and lore which Brown has woven into *The Lost Symbol*. Nor is there anything dry about it; Hall was always the great showman, a master at keeping his audience on the hook by knowing how to tell a good story. His *Secret Teachings* has the quality of a grand narrative filled with numerous tales and vignettes – a modern occult version of *A Thousand and One Nights*, peopled with a fascinating cast of gods and goddess, of magicians, Kabbalists, adepts, alchemists, princes and demons. And perhaps most of all for Brown, the book provokes. As Hall says in his preface to *The Secret Teachings*, 'The entire theory of the book is diametrically opposed to the modern method of thinking, for it is concerned with subjects openly ridiculed by the sophists of the twentieth century'.

This is of immense appeal to Dan Brown who describes himself as a sceptic. He is more interested in the questions than the answers; questioning assumptions has been the key to his attitude on life and and on storytelling. Brown sees Manly Hall as a companion in this venture and has paid him the tribute of prefacing *The Lost Symbol* with an epigraph from *The Secret Teachings*: 'To live in the world without becoming aware of the meaning of the world is like wandering about in a great library without touching the books'. Crucially, those words are part of a puzzle set by Brown, for he leaves it to his readers to discover Hall's next sentence. In whole, what Manly Hall had to say was, 'To live in the world without becoming aware of the meaning of the world is like wandering about in a great library without touching the books. It has always seemed to me that symbolism should be restored to the structure of world education.' That is very Dan Brown.

And finally there is something endearing about Hall with his Hollywood friends and his movie idol looks who nevertheless understood how adulation could turn to disappointment, how easy it was for anyone, including himself, to be seen as a god but then knocked off his pedestal. Hall expressed it touchingly and well when he said, 'Human beings make better humans than they do gods'.

The Founding Fathers

FREE-BORN ENGLISHMEN

'America wasn't founded a Christian country. It became a Christian country. The important thing to remember with the Masons and the Founding Fathers is that many of the Founding Fathers were Deists.'

DAN BROWN, TELEVISION INTERVIEW, 16 OCTOBER 2009

Who Were the Founding Fathers?

Warren G. Harding, who would later become the 29th president of the United States, was still a senator when he stood before the Republican convention in Chicago in 1912 and began one of his characteristically long-winded excursions through American history. 'Human rights and their defence are as old as civilization; but, more important to us, the Founding American Fathers wrote the covenant of a people's rule into the bond of national life, beyond all erasure or abridgment.' Four years later, again at a Republican convention in

THE GREAT SEAL OF THE UNITED STATES

Powerful Masonic symbols have been discerned in the Great Seal of the United States, which is reproduced on the reverse of the dollar bill. The seal was commissioned by Congress on 4 July 1776, immediately after it had voted its approval of the Declaration of Independence, but it would pass through three committees and take six years before a final design was approved. Benjamin Franklin, who was on the first committee, was the only Freemason involved. He was probably remembering his publication of Anderson's Masonic *Constitutions* when he suggested that the seal should depict the Jews escaping from the tyranny of the Pharaoh, but this was rejected. The obverse of the seal shows an eagle clutching thirteen arrows and an olive branch with thirteen leaves and thirteen fruits; the eagle is defended by a shield with thirteen stripes, and above its head are thirteen stars arranged in the form of the Seal of Solomon, also known as the Star of David. Thirteen represents the original thirteen American colonies that rebelled against Britain and came together to form the United States. The motto reads '*E Pluribus Unum*', meaning 'Out of Many, One'. The arrangement of the stars has aroused speculation, but biblical

and Hebrew symbolism and associations were as common in the eighteenth and nineteenth centuries as classical symbolism and associations – explaining, incidentally, why Franklin bore the name Benjamin, why Jefferson's vice president Burr was called Aaron, and why Lincoln's first name was Abraham. Charles Thomson, a Latinist who was Secretary of Congress and the person who set the various ideas for a seal into their final form, explained simply that 'the constellation of stars denotes a new State taking its place and rank among other sovereign powers'.

The reverse of the Great seal shows a pyramid surmounted by an eye. The pyramid has thirteen courses and is inscribed at its base with MDCCLXXVI. There are two mottoes: one above the eye, the other below the pyramid. Charles Thomson gave an explanation: 'The pyramid signifies strength and duration: The eye over it and the motto, *Annuit Coeptus* [He [God] Has Favoured Our Undertakings], allude to the many interventions of Providence in favour of the American cause. The date underneath is that of the Declaration of Independence, and the words under it,

Novus Ordo Seclorum [A New Order of the Ages], signify the beginning of the new American era in 1776.'

But 'alternative histories' and conspiracy theorists see things differently. They say that the pyramid and the eye on the reverse of the Great Seal are Masonic and amount to a code. Expert Freemasons deny this, saying that the seal is not a Masonic emblem, nor does it contain hidden Masonic symbols. Certainly the pyramid is not especially Masonic apart from Freemasonry's occasional taste for Egyptiana, which includes palm trees too. But the eye does figure in Masonic imagery, and it even appears on the Freemason's apron worn by George Washington.

The point, however, is that there is nothing specifically Masonic about the 'all-seeing eye', which was part of the cultural iconography of the seventeenth and eighteenth centuries. For example, in 1614 the frontispiece of Sir Walter Raleigh's *History of the World* showed an eye in a cloud labelled 'Providentia' overlooking a globe. Nevertheless, for those given to conspiracy theories the meaning lies elsewhere. For Robert Langdon, racing around in Dan Brown's *Angels and Demons*, '*novus ordo seclorum*' translates as 'new secular order'. For others it prefigures the 'new world order' announced by George H.W. Bush before a joint session of Congress, after Saddam Hussein had invaded Kuwait and the United States was mustering a coalition to drive the Iraqi forces back. 'Out of these troubled times,' Bush told Congress, 'our fifth objective – a New World Order – can emerge: a new era'. The speech was delivered on 11 September 1990, exactly eleven years before that other '9/11'. Coincidence or what? But there is no such thing as a coincidence, claims Brown.

Chicago, he dropped the 'American' between 'Founding' and 'Fathers' and created an enduring alliterative phrase: 'We ought to be as genuinely American today as when the Founding Fathers flung their immortal defiance in the face of old world oppressions and dedicated a new republic to liberty and justice.' That is when the phrase came about. Not back at the time of the American Revolution, and not even within the lifetimes of anyone who could remember the men who made the revolution. Only long after the event did the Founding Fathers enter the political vocabulary, giving rhetorical power to a long-developing myth. The religion of America *is* America, and its gods are the Founding Fathers. But they are gods created in the shifting image of succeeding generations of Americans who know little about the minds and beliefs of free-born Englishmen (to use the phrase that Benjamin Franklin applied to his countrymen).

The term having been coined, it needed to be determined who actually qualified as a Founding Father. Their number runs from the hundreds to the thousands according to the many different lists. But everyone agrees that the signatories of the Declaration of Independence are Founding Fathers, who include Benjamin Franklin, John Adams and Thomas Jefferson. And also signatories of the Constitution, which brings in George Washington – if his generalship throughout the War of Independence was not qualification enough. These are the four figures that Dan Brown singles out for mention in *The Lost Symbol*, along with Thomas Paine, the brilliant English propagandist, who is always included among the Founding Fathers, even though many Americans would rather forget at least half of what he said.

Dan Brown speaks of the Founding Fathers' distrust of the Bible, of their Deistic beliefs and their Masonic dreams. 'The Founding Fathers had envisioned America as a blank canvas' Dan Brown writes in chapter 133, 'a fertile field on which the seeds of the mysteries could be sown'. So what did those Founding Fathers, the ones Dan Brown mentions by name, really believe?

Benjamin Franklin

Some mention has already been made of Benjamin Franklin's career and his association with Freemasonry (see p.50). Here we will look at his religious beliefs. Franklin was born in 1706 into the Puritan environment of Boston, Massachusetts. The Puritans had come to America for religious freedom, which too often meant their freedom to impose their intolerant beliefs on others. He attended the Latin School, favoured by the sons of Puritans intending to enter the ministry, but at the age of ten he was overseeing his own education.

By fifteen, as he wrote in his autobiography, he had become a Deist. 'Some books against Deism fell into my hands. ... It happened that they wrought an effect on me quite contrary to what was intended by them: for the arguments of the Deists, which were quoted to be refuted, appeared to me much stronger than the refutations; in short, I soon became a thorough Deist.'

At seventeen he escaped to Philadelphia in the colony of Pennsylvania, which had been founded by the Quaker William Penn. It was a very mixed landscape, as described in 1750 by a German traveller: 'Coming to speak of Pennsylvania, that colony possesses great liberties above all other English colonies, inasmuch as all religious sects are tolerated there. We find there Lutherans, Reformed, Catholics, Quakers, Mennonites or Anabaptists, Herrnhuter or Moravian Brethren, Pietists, Seventh-Day Baptists, Dunkers, Presbyterians, Newborn, Freemasons, Separatists, Freethinkers, Jews, Mohammedans, Pagans, Negroes and Indians. The Evangelicals and Reformed, however, are in the majority. But there are many hundred unbaptised souls there that do not even wish to be baptised.'

GREAT AWAKENINGS

The Great Awakening was just then stirring up America, and Franklin reacted to its emotionally charged conversion experiences

Benjamin Franklin, freethinker and Freemason: this portrait by Edward Fisher alludes to his early experiments with electricity.

DEISM

Deism refers to knowing God through the human processes of reason, experiment and observation, as opposed to God revealing himself to man by miracles, messages, visions or through sacred books.

Deism developed in the intellectual atmosphere of the Enlightenment, principally in Britain and France in the seventeenth and eighteenth centuries. It came to America in the early 1730s. It was the cutting-edge view, the one espoused by such people as John Locke and Adam Smith, Rousseau and Voltaire, and it became popular among the educated elite of the British colonies in America. A significant proportion of America's leaders during the revolutionary period were Deists, among them George Washington, Benjamin Franklin, Thomas Jefferson and Thomas Paine.

Deists conceived of God as the creator of the universe, but a God who then steps back and no longer intervenes. They feel admiration for God's creation and find in it a guide to living an ethical life. But, for them, God has laid down no doctrine to follow. He offers no miracles. There is no afterlife. Nor will God respond to pleas or prayers.

But then again, Deism was never a sharply defined and coherent movement, and there were many shades and variations. Some Deists did believe in an afterlife, and some did pray. Deism was sometimes taken as a veiled form of atheism, even though Deism proper recognized the existence of God.

By its intellectual or rational nature, Deism was not an emotional experience. Its tone and thought were in complete opposition to that of the Evangelicals whose fervour first swept America in the Great Awakening of the 1740s.

There was a degree of overlap between Deism and Freemasonry. Many Freemasons were Deists, and also the tolerant stance of Freemasonry made its lodges places where Deists felt comfortable in gathering and discussing their ideas. When Deism came to America it did so at the same time and place as Freemasonry – that is, it arrived in Philadelphia in about 1731. By the early nineteenth century, Deism was on the wane in both Britain and America.

with the greatest distaste. The first of a series of fundamentalist outpourings that would sweep the country at intervals throughout its history, the Great Awakening raged through the Colonies in the 1740s following the revivalism of John and Charles Wesley in England and the visit to America of John Wesley himself, the founder of Methodism, in the late 1730s. The Second Great

Awakening coincided with the Morgan affair, which nearly killed off Freemasonry and also provided much of the emotional energy behind the anti-slavery movement in the run-up to the Civil War; the third Awakening came during the Depression of the 1930s. America has been in the grip of its fourth evangelical spasm since the advent of Jimmy Carter, continuing through the presidency of George W. Bush and the well-publicized sermons attended by Barack Obama, making this a time when it is all but impossible for anyone not publicly and ostentatiously declaring their faith in God to pursue a career in elected office. Dan Brown seems to have been very mindful of this atmosphere, and critical of it, in writing *The Lost Symbol*.

FRANKLIN'S DEISM

Franklin was not a radical Deist, however, and certainly not an anti-Christian one. He believed in a benevolent God, allowed for the possibility of divine intervention, and often went to services at an Episcopal church, though more for the pleasure he took in the ceremony and ritual. He approached the possibility of resurrection in a similar spirit, as shown in an amusing epitaph he wrote for himself when he was a young printer:

The body of
B. Franklin, Printer
(Like the Cover of an Old Book
Its Contents torn Out
And Stript of its Lettering and Gilding)
Lies Here, Food for Worms.
But the Work shall not be Lost;
For it will (as he Believ'd) Appear once More
In a New and More Elegant Edition
Revised and Corrected
By the Author.

Privately, Franklin questioned the Christian doctrines of the resurrection, the incarnation and the Trinity. In public he preferred ambivalence and discretion and, diplomatically, he announced that no one system was entirely right or wrong.

Shortly before his death, Franklin was asked about his religious beliefs. He stated that he believed in one god, the creator of the Universe, and he thought that the soul of man is immortal. Jesus had established the best system of morals known to the world, he said, but Franklin also thought that Christianity had been corrupted since that time and admitted to having 'some Doubts as to his Divinity. 'It is a Question I do not dogmatize upon,' as he went on to say, 'having never studied it, and think it needless to busy myself with it now, when I expect soon an Opportunity of knowing the Truth with less Trouble'. His tolerance and eclecticism did much to swell the large turnout for his funeral in Philadelphia in 1790. None of the Mason fraternity showed themselves (see p.53), but twenty thousand other people did, including all the clergy of the city, representing every faith.

Thomas Paine

Thomas Paine has a claim to the title 'The Father of the American Revolution' because of *Common Sense*, the pamphlet he published anonymously in Philadelphia in January 1776, saying only that it was 'Written by an Englishman'. Within three months, one hundred thousand copies were sold throughout the colonies, which then had a population of about two million, making it one of the first American bestsellers. Until then, and despite such events as the Boston Tea Party and the insurrectionary violence of the Battle of Bunker Hill, public debate about independence had been muted; Paine's pamphlet, with its stinging abuse of the British monarchy – 'Of more worth is one honest man to society and in the sight of God, than all the crowned ruffians that ever lived' – spurred the public mood towards rejection of compromise with Britain and the demand for absolute independence.

Paine was born in Norfolk, England, of poor Quaker parents in 1737. At the age of 35, while working for the British excise service, he wrote his first political pamphlet, *The Case of the Officers of Excise*, which examined the poor living conditions of England's labouring class and demanded more pay for excise officers. Two years later, in 1774, he met Benjamin Franklin in London and was encouraged by him to come to America. Armed with Franklin's introductions, Paine was soon appointed editor of *Pennsylvania Magazine* and became active in the call for American independence. But no sooner had the revolution been won than Paine, too radical for most tastes, fell out of political favour and returned to England.

Paine had many Mason friends, but there is no evidence that he himself ever became a Freemason. He made ample notes and composed the draft of a book called the *Origins of Freemasonry*, which was published only after his death and gives a good impression of his views on the Craft, as well as on Christianity. 'Masonry (as I shall show from the customs, ceremonies, hieroglyphics, and chronology of Masonry) is derived and is the remains of the religion of the ancient Druids; who, like the Magi of Persia and the Priests of Heliopolis in Egypt, were Priests of the Sun. They paid worship to this great luminary, as the great visible agent of a great invisible first cause whom they styled "Time without limits". The Christian religion and Masonry have one and the same common origin: both are derived from the worship of the Sun. The difference between their origin is that the Christian religion is a parody on the worship of the Sun, in which they put a man whom they call Christ, in the place of the Sun, and pay him the same adoration which was originally paid to the Sun.'

Many of the Founding Fathers were either enthusiastic Masons or keen to benefit from visible associations with Freemasonry. By 1933, however, the visit of the Tall Cedars Masonic Order to fellow member President Franklin D. Roosevelt at the White House was considered merely a big PR blunder.

THE AGE OF REASON

The French Revolution soon captured Paine's imagination and he wrote *Rights of Man* in its defence, published in London in 1791, before he went to France to participate in events, only to find himself arrested and imprisoned during the Terror. He would certainly have faced the guillotine but for the fall of Robespierre in 1793. While in France, and afterwards back again in England, he wrote *The Age of Reason*, his argument for Deism, based on a critical examination of the Old and New Testaments, citing numerous contradictions as evidence against a literal interpretation of the Bible. When Dan Brown, in chapter 131 of *The Lost Symbol*, has Peter Solomon say 'It was *here*, Robert, at the very core of this young American nation, that our brightest forefathers – John Adams, Ben Franklin, Thomas Paine – all warned of the profound dangers of intepreting the Bible *literally*', he has *The Age of Reason* in mind.

'Of all the tyrannies that affect mankind, tyranny in religion is the worst. Every other species of tyranny is limited to the world we live in; but this attempts to stride beyond the grave, and seeks to pursue us into eternity.' So Paine sets out his case in *The Age of Reason*, and in his final paragraph he writes: 'I here close the subject. I have shewn in all the foregoing parts of this work that the Bible and Testament are impositions and forgeries; and I leave the evidence I have produced in proof of it to be refuted, if any one can do it; and I leave the ideas that are suggested in the conclusion of the work to rest on the mind of the reader; certain as I am that when opinions are free, either in matters of government or religion, truth will finally and powerfully prevail.'

Despite being invited by no less a person than Thomas Jefferson, the third president of the United States, to return to America in 1802. Thomas Paine's final years in the country which he had helped to bring into the world of free nations were spent penniless and forgotten. These years were the early stages of the Second Great Awakening, another period of great religious revival. Paine's *The Age of Reason* gave ample excuse for the religiously devout to shun him. Ostracized for his criticisms and ridicule of Christianity, only six people attended his funeral. His obituary notice, published in the *New York Citizen* and repeated in newspapers throughout the country, said 'He had lived long, did some good and much harm'.

George Washington

Born in 1732, George Washington was in his forties when he found himself in command of the Continental Army and the nascent fortunes of what would become the United States of America. Washington was less a brilliant general than an unflappable leader of extraordinary tenacity. The integrity of his commitment to what at times seemed a hopeless cause won him that unlimited respect which often was all that held his forces together during America's War of Independence. Unlike other generals of revolutionary armies before and since, he never wavered in his insistence upon respect for civil authority, even in the form of a weak Congress. In 1780, when it looked like victory would go to the British by default, with the Americans barely able to put an army in the field due to mass desertions for want of pay, a delegation from the Continental Congress approached Washington's generals with the proposal that their commander assume the powers of dictator. The proposals never reached Washington's ears, for as General Nathaniel Greene said, 'He has strange notions about the cause and the obligation there is for people to sacrifice fortune and reputation in support thereof. I shall not combat his opinions; but leave time and future events to effect what reason will have no influence upon.' When time came to elect a first president of the United States there was never any question that it should be George Washington. His integrity, his modesty, and his absolute respect for civilian authority in a just cause won him a reputation that has remained unshaken to this day.

Though a place was reserved to receive his remains at the heart of the Capitol Building, the Crypt which Dan Brown imagines was really the site of a modern version of the Vestal Virgins' eternal

THE MYSTICAL CITY? FOUNDATIONS OF THE AMERICAN REPUBLIC

For mythomanes the story of the Freemasons having a determining and mystic hand in the story of George Washington laying the foundation stone of the Capitol Building in Washington DC does not end there. There is far more to it than that. The Capitol was part of the grand plan for the entire city designed in 1791 by Pierre Charles L'Enfant, a Frenchman who served in General George Washington's staff as a military engineer throughout the revolutionary war. Though Washington appointed L'Enfant to lay out the new city, L'Enfant was not a Freemason, but the conspiracy theorists insist he was; and they say that his rectangular street grid overlaid by diagonal avenues creates a series of masonic patterns that also reflect the pattern of the stars. The harmony between the heavens and the earth – as above, so below – would work its powers on those who inhabited the city, the capital of the new republic.

Dan Brown mentions this in *The Lost Symbol*, for example in chapter 6, where he also makes a careless mistake. He says that the city was laid out by three Freemasons, Washington, Franklin and L'Enfant. But not only was L'Enfant not a Mason, but by 1791 Franklin had been dead a year. Furthermore Washington took little interest in laying out the city. Nor did anyone trouble about the position of the stars; in their attempts to make that seems so, occultists and conspiracy theorists are deliberately fuzzy about the times, rearrange people's movements and events, manipulate the facts in such way that everything lines up in some astral way – instead of letting the story fit the facts, they twist the facts to invent a story.

fire, Washington typically preferred to be the private man, so that when he died in December 1799 his wish that he should be buried at his Mount Vernon home was carried out. Washington received Episcopalian and Masonic funerals, both, one feels, as a matter of form and not violating his Deist beliefs.

LIES ABOUT WASHINGTON

But almost since the moment of his death there have been those who for political, religious and moral purposes have embellished Washington's biography with pious lies. There have been very many over the years and the earliest example came the year after his death, with the publication of *The Life of George Washington* by Mason Locke Weems. Kept in print until the 1920s, the biography by Weems became one of the best-selling books in the history of America and was the source for many other works, including a biography of Washington by the future president Woodrow Wilson. The famous story of Washington cutting down the cherry tree and, when questioned by his father, admitting that he had done so, saying 'I cannot tell a lie', was a pure invention by Weems, added only in the fifth edition. In keeping with the early and increasing evangelical mood of America, Weems invented scenes of Washington wandering off into the woods or kneeling in the snow before a battle and crying out to God in anguish. Weems reported how a young girl had unexpectedly come upon Washington at such a moment and overheard him repeat the battle cry from Joshua 22:22, 'The Lord God of gods, the Lord God of gods, He knoweth, and Israel he shall know; if it be in rebellion, or if in transgression against the Lord, save us not this day'.

His body was hardly cold when acquaintances began to report Washington's attention to religion, for example recalling his attendances at church, and the one occasion when he was observed to say grace at table. But Washington's own diaries show that he generally went to church no more than once a month and often much less frequently. Indeed, he was more likely to spend his Sundays visiting relatives and friends or going fox-hunting. Significantly, though raised in the Anglican Church, Washington was never confirmed, and so avoided the sacrament of Holy Communion. Though conscious nearly to the moment of his death, Washington never asked for a clergyman on his death bed.

NOT A CHRISTIAN BELIEVER

In his letters, Washington infrequently used the word Christianity and almost never referred to Jesus Christ. In place of terms like

Saviour, Lord, Redeemer, Washington used the language of Deism, making references to Providence, the Grand Architect, the Author of All Good, the Deity. Washington had no interest in theology or the doctrines of any particular church. President James Madison, who had known Washington well, later said that he did 'not suppose that Washington had ever attended to the arguments for Christianity and for the different systems of religion, or in fact that he had formed definite opinions on the subject'. Bishop William White, the Episcopal cleric who had been chaplain to the Continental Congress and later Washington's pastor during his presidency, made things very clear: 'I do not believe that any degree of recollection will bring to my mind any fact which would prove General Washington to have been a believer in the Christian revelation.'

Episcopalian minister Bird Wilson, professor at the General Theological Seminary in New York, who had known several of the Founding Fathers, and whose own father was himself a Founding Father, gave a sermon in 1831 saying that Washington was not alone among US presidents in his unorthodox beliefs. He claimed that Washington had in fact been a Deist, and moreover that 'among all our presidents downward, not one was a professor of religion, at least not of more than Unitarianism'. The list of names must therefore include Washington, John Adams, Thomas Jefferson, James Madison, James Monroe, John Quincy Adams and Andrew Jackson, that is all the first seven presidents of the United States.

John Adams

The Unitarian in Bird Wilson's list was John Adams, Washington's vice president and the second president of the United States. Years before the Declaration of Independence, Adams made the case for America going its own way, and as a diplomat in Paris he negotiated the Treaty of 1783 which ended the war with England. At Harvard, which he entered at the age of fifteen, he studied Greek and Latin, classical political philosophy, and also science and religion. Adams came as close as any American political leader to fulfilling Plato's wish to see a philosopher in power.

AN ARIAN HERETIC IN THE WHITE HOUSE

Unitarianism has been called Christian Deism. It has also been seen as the successor to the great early Christian heresy called Arianism which challenged the unity of the godhead – the Father, the Son, the Holy Spirit – and opened the way to regarding the nature of Jesus as being not of the same substance as God. Indeed, it lead to the possibility of seeing Jesus merely as a good man, as Unitarians and Muslims see him today.

Adams rejected the Trinity (which put him in line with early Christians, as the doctrine of the Trinity did not evolve until the third century), and he rejected the divinity of Jesus too, as well as the notions of pure evil and predestination. In a letter to his wife, he wrote: 'Let the human mind loose. It must be loosed; it will be loose. Superstition and despotism cannot confine it.' It sounds almost un-American.

Thomas Jefferson

After serving as American ambassador in France, then as secretary of state to George Washington and vice president to John Adams, Thomas Jefferson became America's the third president. During his first term he made the Louisiana Purchase, at a stroke doubling the size of the United States, which now had claims from the Mississippi to the Pacific Ocean. Jefferson was 33 when he wrote the Declaration of Independence. He believed that 'a little rebellion now and then is a good thing'. He could read Latin, French and Italian;

he had practised law; he was designing his own home, Monticello; he had a broad background in philosophy and the natural sciences; and he was an inveterate note-taker, observing that in Philadelphia on 4 July 1776, the temperature at 6am was 68°F, and was 72°F at 9am, 76°F at 1pm, and 73°F at 9pm. In short, he was a brilliantly gifted amateur. About the only thing he was not was a Freemason. In a 1962 speech to a gathering of 49 Nobel Laureates, John F. Kennedy said 'I think this is the most extraordinary collection of talent and of human knowledge that has ever been gathered together at the White House – with the possible exception of when Thomas Jefferson dined alone'.

Jefferson's spiritual views are hardly controversial, simply because nowadays they are so well known, though during his lifetime he took the precaution of appearing outwardly to be an Anglican (or, after the revolution, an Episcopalian). Then, as now, the Anglican/ Episcopalian Church is a broad one. But his views did leak out, not least because of his own publication, *Notes on the State of Virginia*, published in France in 1785 and in England in 1787, in which he opposed religious coercion and established churches, and said that 'millions of innocent men, women, and children, since the introduction of Christianity, have been burnt, tortured, fined, imprisoned'. Jefferson's great ideological rival, Alexander Hamilton, called him 'an athiest in religion and a fanatic in politics'. But it did not stop Jefferson getting himself elected president twice.

REWRITING THE NEW TESTAMENT

As Dan Brown rightly says in *The Lost Symbol*, Jefferson even did a scissors-and-paste job on the New Testament, cutting out all the miracles and the Jesus-as-God bits, including the Immaculate Conception, the Virgin Birth and the Resurrection. Jefferson said 'I found the work obvious and easy'. And he gave it a new title,

An obelisk not a cross was favoured by Jefferson for his self-designed granite monument to himself at his grave at Monticello. This original now rests at the University of Missouri-Columbia after a larger one was built in its place.

The Life and Morals of Jesus of Nazareth. But Dan Brown is wrong in saying that a copy of the Jefferson Bible was presented to every new member of Congress during the first half of the nineteenth century. Jefferson would not allow it to be published in his lifetime; its appearance had to await his grandson, who came to an arrangement with the Smithsonian Institution to publish it in 1895. Nevertheless it is remarkable that by a 1904 Act of Congress the book was reproduced in a lithographic edition which indeed was then given to every new member of Congress for many years – a century after Dan Brown's version of the story.

Dan Brown and the Founding Fathers

One of the themes of *The Lost Symbol* is that man is limited, even crippled and enslaved, by religious doctrines. Dan Brown presumably has in mind the present evangelical mood in America, though in fact it has been a recurrent historical experience, with waves of fundamentalism, called Great Awakenings, washing across the country every few generations. One such wave nearly washed away the Freemasons in the 1820s. Anti-Masonic feeling at that time was touched off by the Morgan affair (see p.58), and probably there was justice in the concern. But the scale of the hysteria was owed to something much greater than that, something far deeper in the American experience. After all, the first settlers in New England, the ones who landed at Plymouth and whom Americans claim as seekers of religious freedom, had a long history of being religious bigots back in England. Indeed when they had their chance in England, after fighting a violent civil war, they had established a Puritan dictatorship run by Oliver Cromwell which busily went about banning theatre, Christmas, indeed anything that might bring joy to people's hearts. It was a relief for England to see these seekers of 'religious freedom' leave for the New World. But the Founding Fathers were not like that, at least not such patrician figures as Washington and Jefferson, nor Franklin who had fled to tolerant Pennsylvania from Puritan-controlled Massachusetts, nor the Englishman Thomas Paine who was a Quaker by background and a true freethinker. All these men were Deists. Dan Brown is saying that their America was not the America of today, and if mankind is to realize its full potential it must return to the tolerant views of the Founding Fathers.

The Science

'The ancient mysteries deal in the concept of the power of the human mind. All of these texts from all of these different authors tend in the same direction. This idea of the power of the human mind and the ability of thought to actually transform the world in which we live.'

DAN BROWN, TELEVISION INTERVIEW, 16 OCTOBER 2009

Noetic Science

Dan Brown says the reason it took him so long to write *The Lost Symbol* was the time it took for him to get to grips with noetic science. He first came across noetics when he was writing *Angels and Demons*; years had passed since then, and when he looked into noetic science again he was struck at how far it had developed. Amazed at its potential, he decided to make it a central theme in his new book.

The term noetic derives from the Greek word *nous*, meaning mind. According to the third century AD Neoplatonic philosopher Plotinus, *nous* is the divine intelligence, the demiurge that is the first emanation from the One. Noetic scientists compare it to intuition, that sense of knowing and connecting which you cannot quite explain but which you sense is real. They also see it as the purely mental ability to control the material world – mind over matter. The science part lies in applying the rigours of observation to see if age-old ideas such as faith healing, telekinesis and extra sensory perception (ESP), to see if they actually have a demonstrable basis in fact. In *The Lost Symbol* Katherine Solomon has a secret laboratory at the Smithsonian Institution, where she conducts pioneering research to discover if the human mind has such powers. When Mal'akh breaks in to kidnap her and destroy her work, he murders her assistant, Trish Dunne. The unfortunate Trish Dunne is actually a tribute to Brenda Dunne, manager of PEAR (the Princeton Engineering Anomalies Research laboratory) – although, thankfully, the real-life Dunne has not been drowned in a tank of liquid ethanol containing a giant preserved squid. PEAR wound up its activities in 2007 but was an inspiration and catalyst for much activity in the field of noetics today. For example, there is the Institute of Noetic Sciences, or IONS, in Petaluma, California, which Dan Brown mentions in chapter 15 of *The Lost Symbol*; Katherine is also described as being fascinated by Lynne McTaggart's book *The Intention Experiment*. McTaggart's website of the same name runs mass experiments to determine if the focused intentions of people can produce a material result. Neither McTaggart nor Marilyn Schlitz, the director of IONS, are exactly wallflowers when it comes to suggesting that they are the models for Katherine Solomon.

THE PRINCETON ENGINEERING ANOMALIES RESEARCH LABORATORY

The Princeton Engineering Anomalies Research Programme (or PEAR, as it is endearingly known), was established at Princeton University in 1979 by Robert Jahn who was then Dean of the School of Engineering and Applied Science. The purpose of PEAR was to conduct experiments under scientific conditions into the possibility of human consciousness having an effect on matter and events. The tests were done using random number generators (RNGs). They were like coin-flippers, producing binary heads or tails results in a random fashion, and were able to do so millions of times, with a truly random result producing fifty percent heads, fifty percent tails. Participants in the experiments were then instructed to concentrate on trying to alter the result in favour of either heads or tails.

In one of the tests regarded as most successful by PEAR over the course of millions of trials, a result was obtained of 50.02 percent for heads. One operator, however, who was used in 23 percent of the trials, is believed to have been a PEAR staff member (although PEAR have not said). Her hit-rate was 50.05 percent, and if her results are not included, the overall result drops to 50.01 percent. PEAR claimed that either figure would be significant, as it is not exactly 50 percent, but critics say that operator bias can play a part in the results, and that, furthermore, the RNGs themselves cannot be assumed to produce perfectly random results.

Throughout its 28 years of existence, PEAR regularly attracted criticism from scientific and academic quarters for flawed procedures and uncritical interpretation of its own data. According to Robert Lee Park, emeritus professor of physics at the University of Maryland and a former Director of Public Information at the American Physical Society, the slightest imperfection can produce more than 50 percent heads (or tails), and the PEAR studies were filled with statistical flaws. One of the ways PEAR made nonsense of their results was by meta-analysis.

Interestingly, Dan Brown repeatedly refers in awestruck tones to the metasystems analysis carried out by his character Trish Dunne, named after Jahn's assistant Brenda. A metasystem is a system created out of several systems. But an analysis of a metasystem has value only if the separate systems are meaningfully related to one another. The birth rate in India and rainfall in the Sahara can each be meaningfully analysed, but analysing them together is meaningless. That in effect was what PEAR was doing in some of its analyses; it was amalgamating results from separate and very different tests with the effect of producing a meaningless overall result. 'It's been an embarrassment to science, and I think an embarrassment for Princeton,' said Professor Park, who is the author of *Voodoo Science: The Road From Foolishness to Fraud.* 'Science has a substantial amount of credibility, but this is the kind of thing that squanders it.'

It was precisely that Jahn and Dunne were operating PEAR under the aegis of Princeton University that accounted for much of their credibility in the outside world. But Princeton was not paying for PEAR, nor was any other academic body or the government, as would normally be the case. Jahn, who had been an aircraft engineer, persuaded his friend James McDonnell, founder of the McDonnell Douglas Corporation, a major civilian and military aircraft manufacturer, to pump millions of dollars into PEAR. Another major backer was Laurance Rockefeller, who happened to have financed the McDonnell Corporation after the Second World War and who also took a lively interest in Unidentified Flying Objects. These were not people who felt a need for scientifically demonstrable results, or who required peer review.

As *The New York Times* reported when PEAR closed down in 2007: 'Over almost three decades, a small laboratory at Princeton University managed to embarrass university administrators, outrage Nobel laureates, entice the support of philanthropists and make headlines around the world with its efforts to prove that thoughts can alter the course of events. Princeton made no official comment.'

In 2005 Brenda Dunne received the Pigasus Award. Not Pegasus, the flying horse, but a plaque bearing the relief of a flying pig. Formally known as the Uri Award, after Uri Geller, it was awarded to Dunne in her capacity as Princeton Engineering Anomalies Research lab manager 'for the doublespeak of promoting studies whose "experimental results display increases in information content that can only be attributed to the influence of the consciousness of the human operator", while simultaneously insisting that PEAR is "not in the business of demonstrating 'paranormal' abilities".'

THE INSTITUTE OF NOETIC SCIENCES

Marilyn Mandala Schlitz, who has only recently added Mandala to her name, is the director of the Institute of Noetic Sciences in Petaluma, California. IONS has an isolated laboratory which is something like Pod 5 in *The Lost Symbol* where, like PEAR, she conducts experiments using Random Number Generators; she also has people stare at freezing water to see if they can affect the formation of ice crystals. The Institute undertakes research into such subjects as meditation, consciousness, alternative healing, spontaneous remission, psychic ablities and survival of consciousness after death.

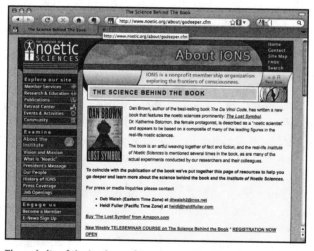

The website of the Institute of Noetic Sciences. Keen to promote *The Lost Symbol* association, among the site's numerous links it currently offers a course on the 'science behind the book'.

Schlitz has no trouble seeing herself as Katherine Solomon. 'Short of olive colored skin, long hair, a wealthy family, and a crazy sociopath pursuing her, there are some exceptional similarities in our mutual bios. ... I am pondering what it means to become a fictional character in a book that has captured the collective imagination like wildfire on a hot summer day. ... Both Katherine and I know the value and the urgency of our studies. ... We believe that consciousness matters, now and in the future!'

IONS owes its founding in 1973 to the Apollo 14 astronaut Edgar Mitchell, who had an epiphany when returning to Earth from outer space. In the tradition of those who have been initiated into the Mysteries, he said, 'The presence of divinity became almost palpable, and I knew that life in the universe was not just an accident based on random processes. The knowledge came to me directly'.

The University of Virginia, which was founded by Thomas Jefferson, runs a Religious Movements Homepage Project in which it investigates and comments on religious groups and movements. The Institute of Noetic Sciences is one of the groups they follow. 'The Institute seems to see itself as unswervingly secular. The Institute claims boldly in the first lines of its webpage in the "About" section that "We are not a spiritual sect."' Nevertheless the University of Virginia's Religious Movements project classifies the institute as a 'quasi-religious group', saying that 'Even a brief examination of the Institute of Noetic Sciences reveals that it has some spiritual undertones. In the previous quotation the president mentions "multiple realities", "extraordinary states" and "spirit communication". Certainly this is not the language of a fully secular organization.'

There is nothing wrong with being a religious or quasi-religious organization, and many of the world's greatest hospitals and research centres have been founded by and are run by people with a commitment to their faith. But it is a serious problem if an organization fails to realise that its spiritual mindset might affect the clarity of what it describes as scientific research.

That matter is addressed by Quackwatch, which describes itself as a 'guide to Quackery, Health Fraud and Intelligent Decisions'. *The Rough Guide to the Internet* calls Quackwatch 'a good place to separate the docs from the ducks'. In performing that task, Quackwatch has examined the claims and operations of the Institute of Noetic Sciences and has placed it on its list of Questionable Organizations.

THE INTENTION EXPERIMENT

Like Mandala Schlitz, Lynne McTaggart has no doubt that she is Katherine Solomon. 'Every so often', she has written on her blog, 'my life takes such a fantastical turn that I am overwhelmed by the feeling that I am actually in the midst of a lucid dream, and that any moment awakening will hand me back my ordinary world. I had that feeling yesterday when I got an email from my editor informing me that my book *The Intention Experiment*, my website: www.theintentionexperiment.com and a good deal of my research were named, explained and used as the background source of a major plotline in Dan Brown's new book.' The black-haired fifty-something McTaggart, who is also the author of *The Field: The Quest for the Secret Force of the Universe*, goes on to note that Katherine Solomon is a noetic scientist, 'a 50-year-old black-haired woman who has written two popular books about the new science of consciousness and the bridge between science and spirituality, which "established her as a leader in this obscure field". Presently she conducts mind-over-matter research and is particularly interested in the power of group minds to change the physical world. At this point, the story began to sound strangely familiar.'

A journalist by trade, McTaggart uses her website and her international readership as a 'global laboratory' to test the power of thought. So far she has conducted nineteen experiments, testing whether group thought can increase the growth of plants, change essential properties of water and living things, clean up polluted water and lower violence in a war-torn area. These experiments have attracted as many as fifteen thousand people at a time from ninety countries round the world, who all follow McTaggart's instructions to send the same thought at exactly the same moment, usually for ten minutes. According to McTaggart, the results have been impressive and go far beyond anything that could be ascribed to chance.

Other successes have included the case of a construction site worker whose hand was badly burned in an accident. He decided to receive 'intention' from McTaggart's followers rather than be treated at hospital – unlike a work colleague of his who had received similar burns. 'Astonishingly, his hand dramatically improved in six days – weeks before that of his work colleague – and was considered by his doctors a medical miracle.'

And then there was the woman who had lost sight in one of her eyes; the following day she told McTaggart and her group that 80 percent of her sight had been restored. McTaggart arranges an 'intention of the week' which involves each participant choosing a special intention space, powering up through meditation, moving into a state of peak focus, making one's intention very specific and visualizing the intention as established fact. The 'intention of the week' as this book is going to press is directed at 'Dan Paho – Help him get a job to support his young family'. People can drop in to the centre and ask to be intentioned, like one young man who wants to be taller. Or the girl quoted on the website making the following appeal: 'I want to be able to achieve my dreams, I don't want to feel overwhelmed by the simplest tasks. It feels like I'm always in a quest to find out a way to fix me, my body, my thoughts, my beliefs. Please, if you can, send some positive energy this way.'

McTaggart has also developed a technique for sending intentions by email. Power up, embed your intention in a word (any word will do), include the word in your email, and send it to a friend. The energy it contains will have its effect at the time intended by the sender, regardless of when the email was sent or where it was sent from.

This might be what Robert Langdon realized it was all about when he stood atop the dome of the Capitol in that bright Washington dawn and 'felt a powerful upwelling deep within himself' – the 'emotion he had never felt this profoundly in his entire life'. Could it have been Lynne McTaggart intentioning him with Hope?

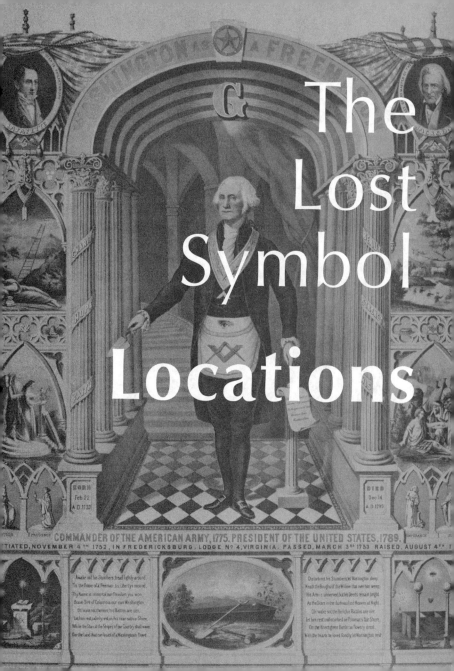

The Lost Symbol Locations

Where the action is

AND HOW TO FIND IT

'Washington, DC has everything that Paris, Rome and London have in the way of great architecture, great power bases. Washington has obelisks and pyramids and great art. And a whole shadow world that we really don't see.'

DAN BROWN, INTERVIEWED BY MATT LAUER, 15 SEPTEMBER 2009

Dan Brown couldn't have picked a better setting for *The Lost Symbol* than Washington, DC. It's the capital of a nation that is home to two million of Freemasonry's five million worldwide members. And the city was sited and planned with the cooperation of George Washington, who was a Freemason himself.

From the Executive Branch to Congress and the courts, the US capital has been overseen and ruled by numerous adherents to the fraternal order – at least 14 of the 44 presidents have been members. The hallmarks of Masonry can be found almost everywhere across the city, from the actual Masonic lodges that make appearances in the novel, to former sites of temples now occupied by museums (such as the National Museum of Women in the Arts; see p.180).

Freemasonry, say enthusiasts, has informed the placement and shape of other major buildings in the city and even the currency in American wallets – the one-dollar bill is adorned with as many mystical symbols as those tattooed on the severed hand of Peter Solomon.

In fact, Brown's biggest challenge may be less in persuading readers of the Freemasons' deeply rooted presence in DC than in trying to convince us that it is somehow secret. What follows is a description of the major sites of Masonic Washington, most of them found within *The Lost Symbol*. But we also visit a few other sites that will reward a visit if you're interested in fully immersing yourself in Robert Langdon-style symbol-sleuthing.

Masonic Monuments

Although many of Washington's sights may have a Masonic connection to some degree, there are some structures whose construction owes much more to the Order of Freemasonry proper. Dan Brown is meticulous in describing some of these, though there are still a few sites beyond those mentioned in *The Lost Symbol* that may merit a look if you're particularly intrigued by the secret society, and wish to understand some of the commonalities of Masonic design close-up.

Keep in mind, though, that however much conspiracy theorists would like to believe it, there is no singular hierarchy of Masons in the city or the country – there is no Grand Mason at the nexus of the brotherhood, or any other spiritual top man calling the shots. Rather, each state and lodge sets many of its own rules.

While all American Masonic orders require belief in a supreme being (Christian or otherwise), they also, by contrast, steer away from discussion of divisive issues such as politics and religion. It's an informal policy that no doubt has had much to do with the organization's staying power over the course of more than three hundred years.

Scottish Rite Temple

John Russell Pope's Scottish Rite Temple, also known as the 'House of the Temple', is located halfway between Downtown and the Shaw district (1733 16th St NW; Mon–Thurs: library and museum

The striking Masonic imagery on the window of the Pillars of Charity room, in the House of the Temple.

The Temple Room altar in the House of the Temple, scene of both Mal'akh's initiation and his demise.

10am–4.30pm, tours on the hour 10am–4pm; ☎202/232-3579, Ⓦwww.srmason-sj.org). It's one of DC's most eye-catching buildings; indeed, in the 1930s the American Institute of Architects voted it one of the five finest structures in the world. If you're anywhere in the vicinity, you can't possibly miss it. Its towering Ionic columns, ziggurat-like roof and huge base are part of an overall design inspired by the Mausoleum at Halicarnassus, one of the Seven Wonders of the Ancient World. Built in 1915 out of limestone and granite, the Masonic temple is, as you would expect, loaded with arcane symbolism, striking imagery – notably the twin sphinxes guarding the place at the front – and inscriptions that propound Masonic ideals of knowledge and truth.

Not surprisingly, the Temple is first among the Masonic locations visited by Dan Brown in *The Lost Symbol's* whistle-stop tour of Washington. Within this 'colossal edifice', Mal'akh is initiated into the Masonic brotherhood in the first pages of the book in the building's imposing Temple Room, and that same room's glass oculus is shattered, in true Hollywood action-movie style, by the UH-60 helicopter in the novel's climactic scene.

In chapter 30, Brown likens the building to 'a classical masterpiece, whose symbolic ornamentation rivalled that of Scotland's Rosslyn Chapel' (which appears in *The Da Vinci Code*) and later, in loving detail, he pores over its Temple Room (chapter 115), main atrium (chapter 124), Hall of Honor (chapter 124) and Masonic chair (chapter 131). It's not surprising that Brown can't resist a last scene in the building's library, DC's oldest public reading room.

Unlike many such temples, this one has long been open to the uninitiated. There's a museum that honours the works of selected Masons, both locally and nationally, and which shows off a selection of regalia that includes the ceremonial vestments of each degree of Freemasonry, such as aprons, caps, jewels, rings and so forth – the higher the rank, the more elaborate the costume.

The imposing George Washington Masonic memorial. Its 333-foot tower was modelled on the Lighthouse of Alexandria, one of the Seven Wonders of the Ancient World that has not survived.

Pride of place, however, goes to the replica of the foundation stone of the US Capitol, laid by George Washington in 1793, a nearly perfect 18-inch cube that modern archaeologists still have not located. The public library also rewards a visit, housing a voluminous collection of works by Robert Burns, the Scottish Mason and poet. The temple is open for daily tours, and its staff will likely have ready answers to many of your *Lost Symbol* questions, though you'll probably get short shrift if you start asking about secret rituals and handshakes.

GEORGE WASHINGTON MASONIC MEMORIAL

In an area bursting with Washington mementos, few are more striking than the George Washington Masonic Memorial, across the Potomac River in Alexandria, at 101 Callahan Drive (daily: summer 9am–4pm, winter 10am–4pm; ☏703/683-2007, Ⓦwww. gwmemorial.org), whose 333-foot tower – built on top of a Greek-style temple – looms behind the King Street Metro station, where CIA agent Simkins makes a fruitless trip in chapter 78. The Virginia Freemasons built the memorial in 1932 to honour a 'deserving brother' and the tower was designed to resemble nothing less than the long-destroyed Lighthouse at Alexandria, another one of the Seven Wonders of the Ancient World.

Brown's short description of the monument is tantalizing, calling it a symbol of 'man's intellectual ascent' (chapter 76). He includes plenty of details about the building, such as its 17-foot-tall bronze statue of George Washington in Masonic garb and treasures such as a 'replica of the Ark of the Covenant' that make you almost wish the action had paused there for longer. Other sundry memorabilia and dioramas at the monument depict events from Washington's life, but to see these, and the superb views from the observation platform, you'll have to take a forty-minute tour, which leaves from the building's main hall (daily 10am, 11.30am, 1.30pm and 3pm).

George Washington's bronze statue, housed within the George Washington Masonic Memorial, Alexandria.

But even from the steps outside, the views across the Potomac to the Washington Monument and Capitol dome in the distance are terrific, well worth the short hop by Metro into Virginia (Blue or Yellow lines; details at ⓦwww.wmata.com).

FRANKLIN SQUARE

Another of Dan Brown's great teases has the CIA chasing off to Franklin Square, where the luckless agent Simkins locates the Almas Shrine Temple, in which he waits to apprehend Mal'akh in chapters 93 and 99. But the action soon shifts to Kalorama (see p.213), and the 'fraternity of philanthropists who wore little red fezzes and marched in parades' – the Ancient Arabic Order Nobles of the Mystic Shrine – are soon forgotten, as is as their mosque-like building.

The Shriners, who are based at 1315 K Street NW – a members-only building – epitomize Brown's vision of Freemasonry as a welcoming organization that embraces many types of spiritual communities. Shriners are best known for their charitable work supporting children's hospitals, and their temples can be found across the US. However, the building's exotic Moorish façade is just that – a façade. The Society is not Islamic in any way and the Middle Eastern trappings might arguably be traced back to the nineteenth-century Orientalist fad and its appetite for exotic ritual, though the building itself dates from 1929. As for the square itself, located in downtown DC between 13th and 14th streets, it's a large, inviting, tree-covered expanse broken up by paths, benches and a central fountain. It's overlooked by the Victorian-era, red-brick Franklin School, the place where Alexander Graham Bell sent his first telephone message.

OTHER MASONIC HIGHLIGHTS

Since Washington, DC figures so prominently in the American Masonic world, there are plenty of worthwhile edifices and museums to see and explore, and it's no wonder that Dan Brown didn't have time to include them all. However, if you're doing the full Freemasonry tour, you'll no doubt want to hit some of the following if you have the time.

The easiest stop-off is the centrally located Judiciary Square. It's just north of Capitol Hill and is bordered by 4th, 5th, D and F streets, around which much of the DC bureaucracy sits. It features a statue of legendary Supreme Court justice John Marshall, as well

LANGDON'S ROUTE

On the inside covers of this book, you will find the map for this route, with the location of the sites in bold. See also the Washington, DC map on pp.210–211 for outer locations, and the Washington Metro map on p.206.

1. Langdon is driven in from DULLES INTERNATIONAL AIRPORT. Brown refers to the crossing point as the 'Memorial Bridge'. Though there is more than one bridge across the Potomac incorporating the word memorial, it is highly probable that he is referring to the ARLINGTON MEMORIAL BRIDGE – despite saying that, to his left, Langdon can see the TIDAL BASIN and the JEFFERSON MEMORIAL. (These would be on his right.) Nevertheless, as Brown makes clear, Langdon is headed directly towards the LINCOLN MEMORIAL and in the distance he can see the Washington Monument. Once Langdon's taxi has crossed the bridge it comes up close to the Lincoln Memorial. Brown doesn't indicate Langdon's route to the CAPITOL BUILDING from here but it is likely that it was via Constitution Avenue or Independence Avenue.

2. Due to security precautions around the CAPITOL BUILDING, Langdon is dropped by his limo at some distance from it and walks.

3. From the Capitol Building, Langdon is guided by Warren Bellamy along the underground tunnel from the Capitol Building to the JEFFERSON BUILDING of the LIBRARY OF CONGRESS. Katherine meets up with Langdon at the Jefferson Building.

4. Langdon, with Katherine, travels along the book conveyor from the JEFFERSON BUILDING to the Adams Building. Bellamy has stayed behind at the Jefferson Building, before he is caught and is taken to the BOTANIC GARDEN for interrogation.

5. Langdon and Katherine leave the ADAMS BUILDING by a side entrance and find themselves outside the FOLGER SHAKESPEARE LIBRARY immediately

as a bearded, imposing Albert Pike. The latter is a rather curious figure to be in such a prominent location, as a member of the anti-Catholic Know-Nothing Party, a Confederate general charged with scalping war captives, and an all-around advocate and enthusiast for slavery. However, after the Civil War he was mostly known for his Masonic writings, which included *Morals and Dogma of the Ancient and Accepted Scottish Rite of Freemasonry*, which is a commentary on the thirty-two degrees of Scottish Rite Freemasonry. Indeed, in some

north of the Adams Building.

6. From the Folger they walk to the corner of 3rd Street and East Capitol Street looking for a taxi.

7. Langdon and Katherine walk up 3rd Street where they catch a taxi. They tell it to head northwest, towards **UNION STATION** and along Massachusetts Avenue.

8. At some point during their taxi ride, Katherine realizes that the driver has tipped off the CIA about his passengers. So Katherine insists they change course and go to **FREEDOM PLAZA** at Pennsylvania Avenue and 13th Street. They probably undertake this route from Union Station by travelling west along E Street NW.

9. Having loudly told the taxi driver that they are going to take the Metro to King Street Station, Katherine and Langdon enter the **METRO CENTER STATION** – but head northwest to **TENLEYTOWN METRO STATION**, not south (see Washington Metro map p.206).

10. Walking from Tenleytown Metro Station, Langdon and Katherine go to the **WASHINGTON NATIONAL CATHEDRAL** (see Washington, DC map). Later they are driven to **KALORAMA HEIGHTS**. While they are at Kalorama Heights, the CIA have gone to Franklin Square.

11. Langdon, Katherine and others arrive at the **HOUSE OF THE TEMPLE**, 16th and S streets. The opening scene of the book also takes place here, where Mal'akh is raised to the Thirty-third degree.

12. Langdon, blindfolded, is taken to the **WASHINGTON NATIONAL MONUMENT**. He is driven there, but Dan Brown doesn't indicate the route.

Finally Langdon and Katherine return to the Capitol Building, where they go up into the dome and out beneath the Statue of Freedom.

people's minds at the time he was virtually synonymous with the Order. Appropriately, after he died his remains were interred in the House of the Temple itself.

Ten blocks northwest, at 1250 New York Ave NW, the National Museum of Women in the Arts (Mon–Sat 10am–5pm, Sun noon–5pm. $10; ☎202/783-5000, Ⓦwww.nmwa.org) occupies the site of a former Masonic temple dating from 1908. It is on the National Register of Historic Places for its trapezoidal shape, cream-coloured pilasters and columns, elegant ground-level arches and upper-storey frieze. It's more than a little ironic that one of the prime buildings of Freemasonry, an organization that resolutely refuses to admit women to its ranks, is now occupied by an institution celebrating the advancement of women in art and culture – and whose inductees would have been refused entry to this or any other temple. Masonic or not, the place deserves a visit, as it houses more than 3500 works by some 700 female artists from the sixteenth century to the present day, as well as silverware, ceramics, photographs and other items.

Of the numerous active temples and lodges around the city, one of the more interesting is Naval Lodge No. 4, located at 330 Pennsylvania Ave SE. It's the oldest Masonic edifice in Washington that maintains its original function. Sited near Capitol Hill and popular with presidents and politicians throughout its history, the lodge dates from 1895 (though the local organization it houses goes back nearly a century earlier) and presents a handsome, late-Victorian façade, its blue interior walls dotted with Masonic imagery and symbols. The general public, however, is not admitted beyond the lobby, unless you happen to be a Mason yourself.

Other notable Masonic sights nearby include: the Grand Lodge of the District of Columbia at 5428 MacArthur Blvd NW, which operates its own Freemasonry-oriented museum and library (entry by appointment only, ☎202/686-1811); the Prince Hall Grand Lodge of the District of Columbia, 1000 U Street NW (members only), heir to a tradition of African-American lodges in the city that goes back to 1825; and the Collingwood Library and Museum, 8301 E Boulevard Drive, Alexandria (Mon & Wed–Sat 10am–4pm, Sun 1–4pm; free; ☎703/765-1652, Ⓦwww.collingwoodlibrary.com), operated by the National Sojourners, an organization for Master Masons who also served as officers in the US military. The Collingwood is a Colonial Revival mansion that is proudly dedicated to what it calls 'Americanism' and holds some 4500 volumes on the nation's history and culture, among them a near-complete set of the writings of George Washington.

The US Capitol

The towering, rib-vaulted dome of the US Capitol soars between the building's north and south wings, occupied by the Senate and House of Representatives, the two legislative bodies of Congress. The building, with its grand halls and statues, committee rooms and ornate chambers, is one of the few places in DC where you get a tangible, awe-inspiring sense of the immense power wielded by the nation's elected officials. The Capitol is the only building in the city without an address, as it stands at the centre of the street plan: the city quadrants extend from the building, and the numbered and lettered streets count away from its central axis. For the same reason, the building doesn't have a front or a back, simply an "East Front" and a "West Front".

The Capitol figures prominently in *The Lost Symbol*, beginning with Langdon's arrival in Washington, when he is dismayed to find the taxi drop-off a 'good quarter mile' away from the building (owing to strict security measures) and he's forced to make a run through a typical Washington downpour. But Langdon is impressed with the Capitol Visitor Center (see below), and Brown reports he would usually have spent 'a full hour' there 'to admire the architec-

The imposing grand exterior of the Capitol Building, Washington, DC.

ture' despite an 'almost crippling aversion to enclosed spaces' that he acquired in a childhood incident.

Along with commenting on its grandeur and the details of its art and architecture, Brown salutes the building's 'treasure trove of bizarre arcana' – from General Logan's stuffed horse to urban legends of ghosts and black cats – though Langdon dismisses the 'crazy ideas' of conspiracy theorists regarding the layout of both the Capitol and Washington itself.

Dan Brown's take on Freemasonry doesn't deny the astrological underpinnings of the Capitol. It's visible enough in Constantino Brumidi's twelve painted signs of the zodiac along the vaulted corridors of the ground floor of the Senate. But Brown rules out any hint of there being a malign influence to them. If anything, Brown is decidedly charitable compared to some of the Capitol's more vitriolic conspiracy theorists, who have found plenty to pick apart in the building ever since it was built.

Some of the more likely claims are linked to Rosicrucianism, which employs symbolism that overlaps with Masonry, while the more outlandish ideas of the conspiracy aficionados suggest that the Capitol was the nexus of the designs of the Bavarian Illuminati secret society during the Enlightenment – or of various Satanists, atheists and other enemies of Christian America ever since. Even when no conspiracy is invoked, the Capitol seems to attract a lot of hostility from some quarters simply because it's the hub of the federal government, and thus in some people's point of view it's the embodiment of everything supposedly wrong with Washington and big government in general.

THE CONSTRUCTION OF THE CAPITOL BUILDING

'A chaste plan, sufficiently capacious and convenient for a period not too remote, but one to which we may reasonably look forward, would meet my idea in the Capitol.'

GEORGE WASHINGTON, 1792

In 1792, nearly a decade after the Treaty of Paris ended the American War of Independence, the nation's leaders formulated plans for a permanent location for the federal legislature, and opened the design of the seat of that government, the US Capitol, to public competition. Dr William Thornton, an amateur whose grand neoclassical offering

---

VISITING THE CAPITOL

The Capitol Visitor Center provides straightforward access for visiting the Capitol, and a definite improvement on the tiresome queuing, lengthy waits for tickets, and all-round red tape that characterized a visit to the building in previous years. The Center itself is open Mon–Sat 8.30am–4.30pm (closed major holidays; ☎202/226-8000) and admission is free. Although the Capitol doesn't have a street address, the Visitor Center is easily found on the building's East Front, across First Avenue NE from the Supreme Court and Library of Congress. For a free tour of the Capitol which includes highlights such as National Statuary Hall and the Rotunda, you'll need an advance online reservation through ⓦwww.visitthecapitol.gov, or, if you're a US citizen, you can reserve through the office of your home-state representative or senator. A small number of same-day tour passes are also provided through information desks on the lower level of the Visitor Center, though you'll want to arrive early in the day for a chance of grabbing one.

Finally, if you feel like braving additional security beyond the already rigorous measures of the Visitor Center, entry into the chambers of the House of Representatives and the Senate requires a fair amount of frisking and scanning, although it may be worth it to see the legislative machinery of the government at work. The only downside is that you can only get a visitor pass (one for each chamber) through the local or Washington, DC office of your home-state representative or senator; foreign visitors can also try to request a pass through their home country's embassy in Washington.

had a splendour deemed appropriate for Congress's meeting place, won the competition. In a ceremony rich with Masonic symbolism, the cornerstone of the Capitol, engraved with a square and compass, was laid by second-term president George Washington on 18 September 1793. By the time the government moved to DC seven years later, however, the Capitol was nowhere near completion.

When Congress assembled for the first time in the brick-and-sandstone building on 22 November 1800, only a small north wing was ready, housing the Senate Chamber, the House of Representatives, the Supreme Court and the Library of Congress. Thomas Jefferson (the first president inaugurated at the Capitol) appointed the respected Benjamin Latrobe as surveyor of public buildings in an attempt to speed up work, and by 1807 a south wing had been built for the House of Representatives, along with a second floor to the north wing, with chambers for the Supreme Court and the Senate. This new construction didn't last long, as British troops burned down the Capitol and the White House in 1814.

With President Madison having fled Washington, the future of the city was uncertain, and some argued for reinstating capital status to Philadelphia. Latrobe himself proffered some grandiose ideas for rebuilding and expanding the Capitol, but they found few admirers, and in 1817 he was replaced by Charles Bulfinch. Reconstructed wings of the Capitol opened again in 1819 and in 1826 the building finally appeared in a form that Thornton might have recognized, complete with a central rotunda topped by a low wooden dome clad in copper.

By the 1850s Congress had again run out of space, and plans were laid to build magnificent, complementary wings on either side of the building and to replace the dome with something more substantial. By 1861, the Civil War threatened to halt work on the dome, but Abraham Lincoln, recognizing the Capitol as a potent symbol of the Union, was determined that the building should be completed.

A cast-iron dome was painstakingly assembled, at three times the height of the previous dome, and in December 1863 the glorious project came to fruition – Brown is totally justified when he remarks that the 'nine million pounds of ironwork in that dome' were 'an unparalleled feat of architectural ingenuity'.

In the next century, surrounding terraces were added, separate House and Senate office buildings were built on either side of the Capitol, and the East Front porch was rebuilt in 1904. The old sandstone columns were replaced 55 years later with marble ones. The East Front was extended in 1962 and faced in marble to prevent the original sandstone from deteriorating further; the West Front – now the oldest part of the building – has so far managed to avoid any modern accretions, though it was restored in the 1980s. Finally, near the end of 2008, the millions of annual visitors to the Capitol were accommodated with an underground visitor centre, which opened to the public just in time to be included in Brown's account of the rich and splendid character of this astonishing building.

CAPITOL VISITOR CENTER

Most visitors' first look inside the building will come via the relatively recently opened Visitor Center. This 'costly and controversial project', as Brown describes it, had a $600 million price tag and long-delayed schedule, which left the East Front of the Capitol resembling a deconstructed shambles for eight years – perhaps symbolically – throughout the Bush administration.

Nevertheless, upon its completion, and blessed with a 'magnificent glass skylight', Brown's take on the Center is that it's an 'underground city to rival parts of Disney World', with over half a million square feet of space for exhibits, restaurants and meeting halls. It might be underground but Brown found the space 'airy somehow'.

The Center features the massive Emancipation Hall which, among other things, contains a plaster cast of the Statue of Freedom (see overleaf), two skylights offering you a chance to experience Langdon's magisterial view of the dome, and around two dozen statues that state governments have donated to the National Statuary Hall but which ended up here, in the overflow space. Among them are figures of Sacagawea and Helen Keller (both icons of women's independence) and Kamehameha I – the first king of Hawaii.

Exhibition Hall is where you can find out all about the building – it houses an eleven-foot model of the dome – and the role it played in the nation's democracy, including biographies and information about some of the key figures in congressional history, and the various inaugurations that have taken place here. There are also the requisite gift shops and restaurants, a pair of theatres devoted to each chamber of Congress, a tunnel to the Thomas Jefferson Building of the Library of Congress, and acres of office space, media production facilities and related infrastructure for politicians and their staffs. Not surprisingly for its cost, the entire below-ground site is huge, occupying up to three-quarters of the Capitol's footprint – making it one of the most sizeable and compelling visitor centres on the globe – and one of the few worthy of extended comment in a top-selling novel.

STATUE OF FREEDOM

When the new, white-painted Capitol dome was inaugurated during the Civil War, hoisted on top of it was the striking, nineteen-foot-high Statue of Freedom by sculptor Thomas Crawford. In the fashion of an ancient Roman resplendent in a feathered helmet and clutching a sword and shield – rather than an American Indian, as popular belief has it – the statue is also known as 'Armed Liberty'.

As Brown writes in chapter 6, setting the scene: 'almost three hundred feet in the air, the Statue of Freedom peered out in the misty darkness like a ghostly sentinel.' He notes how 'ironic' Langdon found it, given its name, that the workers who placed the parts of the heavy statue on its pedestal were slaves.

In fact, while it's true that slaves did construct the Capitol itself, and that they transported and helped assemble the statue's pieces, the actual hoisting was done in 1863 by free labourers – the federal government had expressly outlawed slavery the year before in Washington, DC.

The Statue of Freedom receives a clean. Workers on top of the Capitol Building in 1966 achieved this godlike view of DC using a camera with a fisheye lens attached to a pole.

You can, of course, get the best view of the statue from the exterior balcony just below it, accessed by interior stairs that wind up through the Rotunda past the giant *The Apotheosis of Washington* fresco (see overleaf). This painting has its own balcony 180 feet above the Rotunda floor, or, as Brown describes it, a 'circular catwalk that extended just beneath the ceiling'.

It's where Langdon and Katherine Solomon view 'the fifteen-foot figures that adorned' the dome in chapter 133. Unfortunately, this magnificent view is off-limits to the general public, so unless you happen to be a member of Congress, one of their close friends or perhaps a major campaign contributor, you'll have to be content with Brown's up-close description of the upper dome. Or bring your binoculars.

NATIONAL STATUARY HALL

In *The Lost Symbol*, Langdon looks forward to giving a lecture in what he thinks is 'the best room in all of DC' – National Statuary Hall. And in chapter 8 he finds it 'precisely as he remembered it – a balanced semicircle built in the style of a Greek amphitheatre', with its 'life-size statues of thirty-eight great Americans standing in a semicircle on a stark expanse of black-and-white marble tile'.

Located south of the Rotunda, the Hall is one of the earliest extensions of the building – the 1807 section that once housed the chamber of the House of Representatives. In this D-shaped space, with its stylized coffered ceiling and oculus, the acoustics are such that, from his desk, President John Quincy Adams could supposedly eavesdrop on opposition members on the other side of the room.

After the House moved into its new wing in 1857, the chamber was used for various temporary purposes until Congress decided it should be the dedicated National Statuary Hall. Each state was invited to contribute two statues of its most famous citizens. Three dozen statues are still on display in the hall, with the others scattered around the corridors in the rest of the building, including such figures as Vermont patriot Ethan Allen and Texas revolutionary Sam Houston, missionaries such as Marcus Whitman and Brigham Young, Congressional heavyweights like William Jennings Bryan and Daniel Webster, and, more surprisingly, Confederate rebels including Jefferson Davis.

Since there are exactly one hundred statues in the Hall's collection, the majority can't be shown in Statuary Hall because of space constraints, but you can find the others scattered throughout the building in the Visitor Center, Rotunda, various halls and corridors, and the Crypt.

ROTUNDA

Standing in the Rotunda, you are not only at the centre of the Capitol, but you're at point zero of the entire District of Columbia. William Thornton, the Capitol's first architect, took Rome's Pantheon as his model, so it's no wonder that this is a magnificent space – 180 feet high and 96 feet wide. Langdon 'knew the room was so large that the Statue of Liberty could stand comfortably inside it'. In fact, Langdon runs into the Capitol Rotunda only to witness the commotion surrounding the discovery of Solomon's severed hand.

As the area is sealed off Langdon expands on the theme of Washington's classical heritage, including the Rotunda's link to Rome's pagan Temple of Vesta (a small and now partly ruined building). Solomon's hand points upward to the dome canopy decorated with Constantino Brumidi's mighty fresco *The Apotheosis of Washington* (see box on p.192).

Brumidi had a hand, too, in the frieze celebrating American history that runs around the Rotunda wall, beginning with Columbus's

George Washington as god, or human or both? Brumidi's *The Apotheosis of Washington*.

arrival in the New World and ending with the Civil War. From the floor, it's hard to see much detail of either frieze or fresco, and eyes are drawn instead to the eight large oil paintings that hang below the frieze. Four of the paintings depict European discovery and settlement of the country, in scenes such as Columbus's arrival and the Pilgrims' disembarkation, although the four Revolutionary War pieces by John Trumbull are the most notable.

These paintings date from 1818 to 1824 and are done in the eighteenth-century British vein, with stiff figures and martial pomp and ceremony. Three of them portray military leaders giving up their commands, and one depicts the signing of the Declaration of Independence, showing the key figures who drafted the document – Thomas Jefferson, John Adams and Ben Franklin among them – presenting it to Continental Congress

THE APOTHEOSIS OF WASHINGTON

Sixty-year-old Constantino Brumidi took almost a year to complete his 4600-square-foot fresco of George Washington surrounded by symbols of democracy, arts, science and industry, as well as female figures representing the thirteen original states. The fresco introduces *The Lost Symbol*'s theme that men can become gods, as it depicts Washington ascending freely into the heavens. Early in the novel (in chapters 20 and 21) and at its conclusion (in chapter 133), which takes place on an upper balcony directly beneath the painting, Brown is insistent in advancing the idea that the fresco symbolizes humans' achieving godlike, transcendent status, with Washington as the ideal embodiment of such a notion. However, whether the painting is meant as a literal deification of the first president, a representation of his soul's ascension into a (rather pagan) version of heaven, or an allegory of his immortal standing in history is a question open to debate.

Francis O'Connor, in his exhaustive dissection of Brumidi's work, *Symbolism in the Rotunda*, has the following to say: 'the iconography of the canopy fresco, with its conjunctions of deities and humans, may seem strange to us today. However, in the mid-nineteenth century the personification of abstract ideas by means of figures drawn from classical mythology and the association of historical figures ... was part of the cultural vocabulary. The gods and goddesses stood allegorically for universal virtues embodied in popular historical personalities.'

This isn't exactly Dan Brown-style noetics, exalting the heavenly ascension of humans into gods, but it is a more likely explanation of the complicated iconography employed by the painter. For the complete analysis, see ⓦwww.gpo.gov/congress/senate/brumidi/Brumidi_10.pdf.

president John Hancock, while other legislators stand or sit at rigid attention.

Busts and statues of prominent American leaders fill the gaps in the rest of the Rotunda. Washington, Jefferson, Lincoln and Jackson are all here, along with a modern bust of Dr Martin Luther King Jr and a gold facsimile of the Magna Carta given by the British government. In such august surroundings, more than thirty people – including members of Congress, military leaders, eminent citizens and eleven presidents – have lain in state before burial, almost all of them on the Lincoln Catafalque, a simple pine box shrouded in black that supported the weight of the martyred sixteenth president's coffin in April 1865, and is otherwise housed in a chamber in the Visitor Center. The most recent leader to be honoured in this way was Gerald Ford, who died in 2006 at the age of 93, making him the longest-lived former president. He was also the most recent president to be a Mason.

Capitol Sub-Basement and Crypt

The Capitol sub-basement, according to Brown, can be described as 'ACME storage meets the Catacombs of Domatilla' and contains precisely thirteen storage rooms – a number which has Masonic significance. Some critical action takes place here: it is where Peter Solomon's Masonic altar is discovered and where Langdon tangles with Inoue Sato (and is subsequently saved by Capitol architect Warren Bellamy). The map in chapter 32 of the book gives a sense of the scale of the underground regions of the Capitol – lower realms that are very much part of the book's underworld and intended to be 'very private'.

In fact, although the rooms of the sub-basement are private (as in not open to the public), they are not all that interesting. Most serve as overflow space for House and Senate records and other material and are interconnected by corridors that could only be described as tunnels in the most prosaic sense of the word. Contrary to myth, there are no secret altars, holding pens for UFO wreckage, giant pentagrams or any other fantastic sights jealously guarded by the lucky few who know about them. In fact, with little protest, a good chunk of the sub-basement was summarily wiped out several years ago to make way for the Visitor Center's construction.

More interesting perhaps, and just as subterranean, is the Capitol Crypt. Despite its name, it's not very spooky or secretive either. It's the place where tours from the Visitor Center end: a few offices manage part of the Capitol's bureaucracy, a gift shop sells merchandise, and various exhibits about the Capitol's construction are scattered about, alongside five statues left over from National Statuary Hall. Among these are prominent figures such as Samuel Adams and John C. Calhoun.

Built in 1827 and lined with handsome Doric sandstone columns, the Crypt was designed to be the subterranean floor, directly beneath the Rotunda, that would lead to a lower level housing George Washington's tomb. While it never held the general's body – he's buried with his wife, Martha, at Mount Vernon – the tomb did hold the Lincoln Catafalque (see above) for a number of years, until that was moved to the Visitor Center. Nowadays, the most notable thing about the Crypt is probably the marble compass embedded in the floor marking the exact geographic centre of Washington, DC.

The Washington Monument

A great 'majestic mast of a ship', the Washington Monument is 'the city's centerpiece'. Its 'architectural inspiration was far, far older than the Romans or Greeks', Brown informs us in chapter 3. Standing in the near-centre of the National Mall, the Monument is perhaps the

---

VISITING THE MONUMENT

The Washington Monument can be found at 15th Street NW at Constitution Ave, in the centre of the National Mall, and regular visiting hours are 9am–5pm daily, summer until 10pm (information at ☎202/426-6841 or 1-800/967-2283, ⓦwww.nps.gov/wamo). You can pick up a free ticket from the 15th Street kiosk (on the Mall, south of Constitution Ave; daily 8.30am–4.30pm), which will allow you to turn up at a fixed time later in the day. You'll need to get to the kiosk as early as 7am, as tickets often run out well before noon. You can avoid any disappointment by reserving ahead at ☎1-877/444-6777 and paying a $1.50 service fee per ticket. Upon arrival, you'll be dutifully screened for security – no weapons are allowed of course, but also prohibited are food and drink, backpacks, dogs, and buggies or strollers.

Langdon muses on the city's mystical power as he arrives by jet. Behind the Washington Monument pictured above are the Jefferson Memorial, the Potomac River and the 14th Street Bridge, with the White House in the foreground.

one structure that rivals the Capitol in symbolizing DC.

An unadorned marble obelisk, it was built in memory of America's successful revolutionary general and first president. With its simple, elegant geometry and huge size, it's recognizable from all over the city, providing the capital with a striking central ornament. And of all the novel's Washington locations, none carries the burden of significance more than this towering white pillar, which Langdon first sees from his private jet at dusk as he muses on the city's mystical power.

For him it marks the 'nation's heart' and points him to the final revelation of the illuminated words 'Laus Deo' – of God as a symbol of 'our limitless human potential' – inscribed on the east face of the

THE NOT-SO-SECRET HISTORY OF THE OBELISK

Pierre Charles L'Enfant's original plan for the District proposed the erecting of an equestrian statue of George Washington at the point at which a line drawn due south from the White House would meet one drawn due west from the Capitol – an idea that even the modest Washington approved of. Yet by the time of Washington's death in 1799, no progress had been made on the statue, though a small stone marker was later placed on the proposed spot by Thomas Jefferson in 1804.

The Jefferson Pier, as it is known, is still visible today. Impatient at Congress's apparent lack of enthusiasm for the work, Chief Justice John Marshall and a very aged James Madison established the National Monument Society to foster a design competition and subscription drive in 1833. From this emerged a hugely ambitious scheme from US Treasury architect Robert Mills to top a colonnaded base containing the statues of Revolutionary War-era heroes, with a massive obelisk. The total price tag was $1 million, a huge sum for the early nineteenth century.

Unfortunately, early excavations revealed that L'Enfant's chosen spot was too marshy to build on, and when the cornerstone was finally laid on 4 July 1848, it was on a bare knoll 36 feet east and 12 feet south of the true intersection, which explains why the Monument is off-centre on the map. More trouble arose as political conflicts delayed the construction of the Monument, preventing its completion for decades; it was even likened by Mark Twain to a 'factory chimney with the top broken off'.

When considering the site of the Monument – beside the fetid Washington Canal and often surrounded by cattle awaiting slaughter at a nearby abattoir – the *New York Tribune*, in an almost universally held opinion, condemned it as a 'wretched design, a wretched location'. After the Civil War, Congress finally authorized government funds to complete the Monument and appointed Lieutenant Colonel Thomas Casey of the Army Corps of Engineers to the work.

Casey suffered his own tribulations, not least of which was the discovery that the original marble source in Maryland had been exhausted; you can still see the transition line at 150 feet, where work resumed with marble of a slightly different tone. At long last, by December 1884, the Monument was finally complete.

Appropriately enough for a tribute to a Master Mason, the Monument is the tallest all-masonry structure on the planet. It stands at just over 555 feet tall, measures 55 feet wide at the base, tapers to 34 feet at the top, and is capped by a small aluminium pyramid – with the words 'Laus Deo' sadly far too minuscule to make out even with binoculars.

Monument's pyramidal summit.

Although your views of the obelisk's magnificent silhouette will probably match Langdon's nicely, your experience inside the Monument will likely differ. For one, he rides blindfolded to the top of the obelisk in an elevator (before proceeding down the 896 stone steps of the staircase). Your experience of the tower, however, will first involve strolling up through the concentric stone rings that have been built into the sloping knoll around the Monument (a measure to prevent vehicles from getting too close) before going through the usual security scans.

Once you gain access, the quick, seventy-second elevator ride, best experienced without a blindfold, deposits you at a level of five hundred feet, from where heroic views of the city can be glimpsed through surprisingly narrow windows on all four sides.

There's not much else at the top, other than a replica of the aluminium tip and some other displays, and you'll doubtless be ready to descend within fifteen minutes or so. Unfortunately, going down on foot is not an option, as the stairs have been closed to public access to prevent vandalism, keeping many of the mysterious images and other supposed icons frustratingly out of view.

Back on ground level, an exterior bronze statue of Washington faces east toward the Capitol. Almost seven foot tall, this is a faithful copy of a renowned statue by the eighteenth-century French sculptor Jean-Antoine Houdon that was commissioned for the Virginia State Capitol in Richmond and placed there in 1796. Washington, wearing the uniform of commander-in-chief of the Continental Army, holds a cane in one hand and is flanked by a bundle of rods and a ploughshare signifying, respectively, authority and peace.

If you get to the Monument at dawn, when the interior is closed, you may be able to experience Brown's dramatic account of the structure's illumination, in which 'a tiny speck of golden sunlight was glinting off the highest tip of the towering obelisk'.

Indeed, Brown sees the sun creeping over the horizon and then darkening in reverse at dusk as symbolic: it is like 'the mind of man … receiving enlightenment'. Of all the experiences on a tour of *The Lost Symbol*'s sites, this could be the one that most lives up to its evocative, spellbinding description.

STONES OF THE MONUMENT

During his descent down the Monument stairs, Langdon is very shaken when he spots 'a frightening cloaked figure holding a scythe and kneeling beside an hourglass … pointing directly at a large open Bible, as if to say: "The answer is there!"' This image is actually emblazoned on an honorary stone at the 130-foot level, one of many embedded in the stairway, donated by the Grand Lodge of Maryland in 1850. If anything, Brown's description plays down the strangeness of the figure with the long beard. Not only is he winged, but he has a small plume of hair or perhaps fire erupting from his head. The open book to which he points may or may not be the Bible – it is not clear – and it has a sizeable Masonic square and compass holding down its pages.

This peculiar commemorative block of marble is one of over 200 honorary stones that were contributed by states and private groups in the 1840s, at the invitation of the society that built the Monument (see box on p.196). They wished to drum up enthusiasm for the project and hasten its construction. You can still spot some of these stones on your elevator ride through the structure, though you can't walk past them to view them in close detail as Langdon did, since the stairwell has been closed for decades.

The stones include tributes from various states, foreign countries, militia companies, churches, literary and cultural societies, fire-fighters and fraternal organizations, including numerous Masonic lodges active on the East Coast in the mid-nineteenth century. There are even a few unusual engravings with symbolic Mormon beehives, dedications from defunct temperance societies, and inscriptions from donors such as 'Peter Force', 'Two Disciples of Daguerre' and 'Citizens of the United States in Foo Chow Foo'. One particularly odd stone reads, in Gaelic, 'Our language, our country, our birthplace, Wales forever'.

Of the many donors that took up the society's invitation, the most controversial was Pope Pius IX on behalf of the Vatican – Langdon's old nemesis from *The Da Vinci Code*. The Pope's contribution enraged the Know-Nothing Party, an anti-Catholic, anti-immigrant political movement of the 1840s and 1850s. On the night of 6 March 1854, masked party members stole the Church's donated stone and promptly engineered the organizational takeover of the Monument. Soon after, federal funds for the construction dried up, and Congress refused to provide continuation money as long as the group remained in charge.

Undeterred, the Know-Nothings added several levels' worth of shoddy building and gave the Monument an air of failure for another two decades, leaving it an incomplete stump just 152-feet tall – all thanks to bigoted outrage over a donated piece of marble.

The National Mall

The National Mall is nothing less than the nation's showcase for its most valuable holdings – from the elegant presidential monuments and war memorials along the Reflecting Pool on its western side to the many excellent museums along the grassy eastern side. The Mall runs for two miles, and is bordered by the Capitol at one end and

The Smithsonian Castle: one of several shrines to learning on the National Mall.

SMITHSONIAN PRACTICALITIES

Of the nine excellent Smithsonian Institution museums on the Mall (located between Constitution and Independence avenues west of the Capitol), the original building – known as the Smithsonian Castle – today serves as the main information centre. Ten other Smithsonian sites and museums sit a fair distance from the Mall, either in Downtown DC or as far away as Virginia and New York City.

All the Institution's museums and galleries are open daily all year (except Christmas) from 10am until 5.30pm; some have extended spring and summer hours. Admission is free, though charges are levied for some special exhibitions. For details call ☏202/633-1000 or 633-5285 (Mon–Fri 9am–5pm, Sat & Sun 10am–4pm) or visit ⊛www.si.edu or ⊛www.smithsonian.org.

the Lincoln Memorial at the other. It's really quite a breathtaking stretch, more than meriting Langdon and Katherine Solomon's view of the buildings in the epilogue as 'shrines to man's accomplishments' (just before Langdon's eyes are arrested by the tip of the Washington Monument).

Most of the museums are part of the holdings of the Smithsonian Institution, with the most popular being the National Air and Space Museum and the national museums of Natural History and American History. Each deserves a lengthy visit to see their voluminous galleries and countless treasures if you are in the vicinity.

Late in *The Lost Symbol*, Langdon reflects upon the Smithsonian's values of science, knowledge and wisdom. He's reminiscing about a lecture he once heard by Peter Solomon, himself the Institution's secretary, which took place in the Smithsonian Castle. Brown describes it as a 'Norman Castle' – a rather odd description, for while it does possess a certain medieval flair, the 1855 structure has little of the dour stone heaviness associated with Norman design. Instead, it's a lively neo-Gothic creation of ruddy brown sandstone, sparkling nave windows and slender steeples – more early Victorian fantasy than anything else.

But even the castle can't compete with its neighbour, the Arts

MELENCOLIA I

Dan Brown is meticulous in analysing the arcane meaning of Albrecht Dürer's 1514 engraving *Melencolia I* (see p.115), which has tantalized and tormented art critics and historians for centuries. It's an effect that the artist clearly intended, as the drawing presents so many puzzles, cryptic messages, curious symbols and subtle implications that you could spend a semester in art school – or an entire career – trying to make sense out of it. Among its features are a slumped winged figure surrounded by a bell, dog, hourglass, scales, cherub, ladder, faint skull and various geometric oddments, while the rising or setting sun shines through what may be an arch, rainbow or halo, and the work's flowing title gloriously hangs in the heavens nearby.

Because it is so mysterious, Brown has a field day telling us about the work, which 'depicts mankind's struggle to comprehend the ancient mysteries' and whose 'symbolism is so complex it makes Leonardo Da Vinci look overt'. But his focus is mainly on the mathematical 'Magic Square' shown on the wall, whose various numbers produce the sum 34 and get the reader well into the terrain of mystical numerology. Langdon employs a Masonic cipher to pick apart the meaning of the numbers, eventually arriving at the Latin phrase 'The

and Industries Building. Built in 1881 to house exhibits from Philadelphia's 1876 Centennial Exhibition, its playful polychromatic brick-and-tile pattern is positively jaunty, with all the striking verve of the Gilded Age (the late nineteenth-century, post-Civil War era of prosperity). Unfortunately, it's been closed for several years awaiting a long-overdue interior renovation.

There are a few non-Smithsonian buildings on the eastern side of the National Mall. The US Botanic Garden, 245 1st St SW (daily 10am–5pm; free; ☎202/225-8333, ⓌWwww.usbg.gov), makes an appearance in *The Lost Symbol*: it's the 'living museum' where Warren Bellamy is interrogated by the ferocious Inoue Sato in chapter 74, and it's the one setting in the book where Masonic symbolism is at a minimum.The foliage is a welcome change from Washington's dominant neoclassical splendour. The garden is especially appealing for its 80-foot-tall Palm House, a state-of-the-art greenhouse featuring climate-controlled rooms devoted to colourful ranks of tropical,

One True God', which will have more relevant connotations later in the novel by feeding into Brown's ideas of human empowerment through the mind, its transcendence into the divine, and so on.

In contrast to the author's noetic theories, other recent commentators have seen in the etching Dürer's view of his own depression (thus the title) as seen through astrological symbols, or his angle on contemporaneous political or religious matters, while others tease out readings based on mystical or millenarian Christianity, Greek paganism, various philosophical schools, or, inevitably, alchemy and black magic.

The reality, however, may necessarily be a bit more opaque. Namely, there are aspects of the design – from the surfeit of symbols that almost crowd out the human figures, to the visual contradictions that the artist clearly intended to confound the viewer – that prevent any simple deconstruction that would reveal its full meaning, whether as the hidden answer to the enigma of life, or the obvious plot point in a metaphysical thriller. As with *The Apotheosis of Washington,* there is no single answer or key to the image, and your perspective may be as good as that of any other sleuth of mystery symbols.

subtropical and desert plants. The section showcasing orchids, two hundred varieties of which are visible at any one time, is well worth a visit, as is the Jungle Room, despite the fact that it's humid almost to the point of discomfort due to being stuffed with equatorial trees and other plants.

One of Brown's best jokes in the book is a parodic reference to his own Louvre scene in *The Da Vinci Code*, as Langdon prepares to rush off to the National Gallery of Art to inspect Albrecht Dürer's *Melencolia I* (see box above). Katherine Solomon simply looks up the image on a computer, so we never get a chance to follow the action to the West Building of the National Gallery, where the picture is located.

You, however, need not be so economical. The museum (which isn't part of the Smithsonian) is one of the best in the US, second only to New York's Met in the quality and breadth of its collections. It's divided into a neoclassical west wing and a modern east wing, the latter designed by the Chinese-born American architect I.M. Pei, who also designed *The Da Vinci Code*'s Louvre pyramid.

Not surprisingly, you can't digest all of its stunning Italian, Spanish, French, Dutch, British and American paintings, sculptures and other works in one visit, so plan ahead if you've got limited time in the city. The museum is located on Constitution Ave, between 4th and 7th streets NW (Mon–Sat 10am–5pm, Sun 11am–6pm; free; ☎202/737-4215, ⓦwww.nga.gov).

Around and outside the city

As something of a spiritual travel guide, *The Lost Symbol* presents a broad view of Washington's landmarks and icons, some of which figure prominently in the book, and some of which are merely glanced at in passing by the author. The latter includes the grand neoclassical spaces of Union Station, north of Capitol Hill at 50 Massachusetts Ave NE. Langdon and Katherine are briefly headed there in chapter 76 but they don't arrive, as Omar's cab is diverted and the pair take a train from the central Metro Center stop. To get there they run across Freedom Plaza and throw Omar and the CIA off the trail to King Street Station in Alexandria. The Plaza lies where Pennsylvania Avenue kinks into E Street (at 13th) and is the site of numerous festivals, protests and open-air concerts. Lined in marble, the square is inlaid with a large-scale representation of Pierre L'Enfant's city plan, crafted in bronze and coloured stone.

The CIA play a significant part in the book, of course, and their headquarters, situated out in Langley, Virginia, has its own mysterious symbols. But unsurprisingly, since it's the home office of America's spy bureau, the public is forbidden to take a look. The CIA's website states that there are 'an extremely limited number of visits' that can be undertaken annually for 'approved academic and civic groups'. The website does, however, offer virtual tours, and there you will find some

Freedom Plaza, with Pierre L'Enfant's large-scale city plan underfoot.

information concerning the headquarters and the Kryptos sculpture (if you want to have a go at unravelling its code).

The CIA does also operate a museum of declassified 'artefacts' but once again the virtual tour is the only thing on offer: the public cannot visit, as the museum 'is located on the CIA compound'.

The same holds for one other site that *The Lost Symbol* has helped

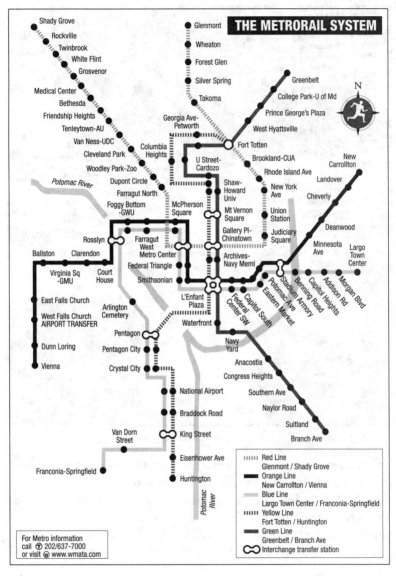

THE METRORAIL SYSTEM

Shady Grove
Rockville
Twinbrook
White Flint
Grosvenor
Medical Center
Bethesda
Friendship Heights
Tenleytown-AU
Van Ness-UDC
Cleveland Park
Woodley Park-Zoo
Dupont Circle
Farragut North
Foggy Bottom-GWU
Rosslyn
Ballston   Clarendon
Virginia Sq-GMU   Court House
East Falls Church
West Falls Church AIRPORT TRANSFER   Arlington Cemetery
Pentagon
Dunn Loring   Pentagon City
Vienna   Crystal City

Glenmont
Wheaton
Forest Glen
Silver Spring
Takoma
Georgia Ave-Petworth
Columbia Heights
U Street-Cardozo
Shaw-Howard Univ
McPherson Square   Mt Vernon Square
Farragut West   Gallery Pl-Chinatown
Metro Center
Federal Triangle
Smithsonian
Archives-Navy Meml
L'Enfant Plaza
Waterfront

Greenbelt
College Park-U of Md
Prince George's Plaza
West Hyattsville
Fort Totten
Brookland-CUA
Rhode Island Ave
New York Ave
Union Station
Judiciary Square

New Carrollton
Landover
Cheverly
Deanwood
Minnesota Ave   Largo Town Center
Stadium Armory   Benning Road   Capitol Heights   Addison Rd   Morgan Blvd
Potomac Ave
Eastern Market
Capitol South
Federal Center SW

Potomac River

National Airport
Braddock Road
Van Dorn Street   King Street
Eisenhower Ave
Franconia-Springfield   Huntington

Navy Yard
Anacostia
Congress Heights
Southern Ave
Naylor Road
Suitland
Branch Ave

Potomac River

N

	Red Line
	Glenmont / Shady Grove
	Orange Line
	New Carrollton / Vienna
	Blue Line
	Largo Town Center / Franconia-Springfield
	Yellow Line
	Fort Totten / Huntington
	Green Line
	Greenbelt / Branch Ave
∞	Interchange transfer station

For Metro information
call ☎ 202/637-7000
or visit ⊛ www.wmata.com

publicize: the Smithsonian Museum Support Center in Suitland, Maryland. The Institution's storehouse is loaded with 54 million items spread out over half a million square feet. In the book, it is where Katherine's noetic science laboratory is housed and where Trish Dunne ends up in a tank with a giant squid – but the Smithsonian is almost as guarded about its treasures as the CIA, and you'll have just as much luck getting in for a browse.

Beyond these, however, there are a few other notable DC sights in the novel that are a little easier to get into.

WASHINGTON NATIONAL CATHEDRAL

The region's most prominent church is Washington National Cathedral (Massachusetts and Wisconsin avenues NW; hours and other information at ☎202/537-6200 or 364-6616, Ⓦwww. cathedral.org/cathedral), which sits on a lofty hill in the Cleveland Park section of town. It is the country's most hallowed site, chosen for the funeral services of presidents and statesmen, with a rich and striking neo-Gothic design, lovely modern stained-glass windows, and a full complement of services and activities that could almost turn you into a full-fledged medievalist. Although officially Episcopal, it's non-denominational Christian for the most part, and plays a key part in the middle section of Brown's novel.

The Cathedral is the only significant exclusively Christian monument to appear in *The Lost Symbol*. However, in the book, Reverend Dean Galloway is, as it turns out, yet another Mason, and he is not entirely on-message with his more zealous Christian colleagues when he offers Langdon more background to the Ancient Mysteries in his office.

Overall, the Cathedral provides a haven of respite amid the chase scenes that take place around it. Its garth (a yard or quadrangle) features a 'cloistered pentagonal garden with bronze postmodern

Washington National Cathedral: one of the novel's less likely sites of Masonic influence.

fountain'; its garden holds a 'gazebo – known as Shadow House [that] sits elegantly amid pathways of stones dug from George Washington's private quarry'; and the nearby College of Preachers

– specifically its kitchen – helps conceal Langdon and Katherine while they hide from the CIA. The Cathedral's environs make for a pleasant setting before the horrors to come at Mal'akh's mansion; and the Cathedral itself is certainly worth a visit in its own right.

The idea of a 'national church' was first proposed by George Washington. But it was not until a century later that Congress finally granted a chapter for what is officially known as the Cathedral Church of St Peter and St Paul, when the foundation stone was laid in 1907. Among US presidents, Woodrow Wilson (who used to visit the construction site in his limousine) is the only one to actually be buried here.

The Cathedral itself was built from Indiana limestone in the English Gothic style, completed with flying buttresses, bosses and vaults and striking stained-glass windows, quirky gargoyles (including Darth Vader, as Langdon discovers to his surprise), massive columns and, as an all-American touch, two rows of state flags hanging below the clerestory level.

Regular restoration projects mean the cathedral always looks stunning. You can visit the cathedral daily on a regular guided tour, but for the speciality tours – exploring such attractions as the gargoyles or the gardens in depth – you should phone ahead or check the website in advance (see p.207).

However, be warned that if you take the Metro to Tenleytown, like Langdon and Katherine, you will have a long mile-and-a-half walk south along Wisconsin Avenue. (There is a slightly shorter stroll from Woodley Park Zoo, turning left from Connecticut Avenue into Cathedral Road and then right into Woodley Road.) If you're not driving, the Cathedral may be easily reached by bus from Pennsylvania Avenue downtown, or from Farragut Square via Dupont Circle and Embassy Row.

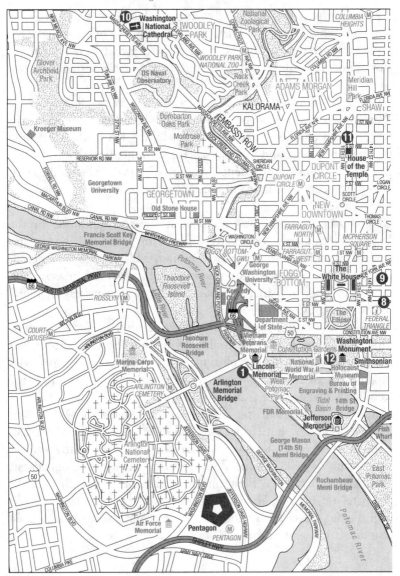

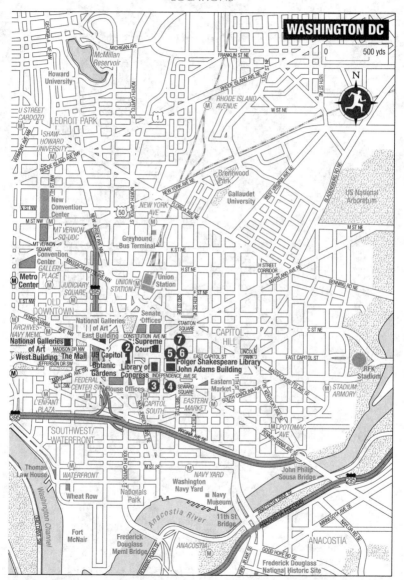

A marble mosaic of the Roman goddess Minerva on a landing above the Library's Great Hall.

KALORAMA HEIGHTS

Near to the Cathedral in *The Lost Symbol* is the lair of the demonic Mal'akh, a little further down the road at Kalorama Heights, located north of Sheridan Circle, where exclusive, quiet streets with manicured lawns stretch out to meet Rock Creek Park. There the diplomatic community thrives behind blinds and bulletproof glass in row after row of multimillion-dollar townhouse embassies, private homes, and hibiscus-rich gardens. Unlike the action of the latter part of the novel, you won't find too much decadence or violence around here. The closest the area has come to any turbulent event in recent history was probably back in 1981 at the Washington Hilton (just east, at 1919 Connecticut Ave NW), where John Hinckley almost ended the life of Ronald Reagan by taking a few shots at the president in the parking lot.

LIBRARY OF CONGRESS

One other significant site in Washington, DC, that figures in the pages of *The Lost Symbol* is the Library of Congress, 1st Street SE at Independence Ave (℡202/707-8000, Ⓦwww.loc.gov). The Library is introduced fairly early in the book: Langdon decides its Reading Room, in the Jefferson Building, might be the most beautiful room in the world, altogether a 'feast for the senses'. The Library features a horned statue of Moses. In case you were wondering why Moses has horns, the book helpfully explains, pointing out how an error in translation can change (cultural) history. It derives from an ancient mistranslation by St Jerome, of the Hebrew for 'rays of light' as 'horns'. Katherine and Langdon later escape underground into the library's Adams Building in chapter 62, though little description is given of its features. As they leave the building by a side entrance they find themselves outside the Folger Shakespeare Library (at

The visual feast that is the Library
of Congress Reading Room.

201 E Capitol St). Dan Brown notes that the Folger is where the 'original Latin manuscript' of *New Atlantis*, the utopian fiction by Sir Francis Bacon, is housed. The work was supposedly the inspiration for American forefathers aspiring to create a new world to be constructed on 'ancient knowledge'.

If you want to explore the Library of Congress in greater depth, there are plenty of opportunities. For one thing the Library is not just a fantastic building but also the nation's official copyright office and the world's largest library – it's said that, on average, ten items per minute are added to its holdings. Books are just part of its unimaginably vast collection. Some 130 million items, from books, maps and manuscripts to movies, musical instruments and photographs, are kept within 530 miles of shelving in closed stacks spread out over three buildings. And there they stay, as the Library of Congress does not circulate its materials beyond the complex.

Any visit ought to include the Great Hall, rich and awe-inspiring with its marble walls and numerous medallions, inscriptions, murals and inlaid mosaics. And the octagonal marble and stained-glass Main Reading Room, more than deserving of Brown's praise, is a beautiful galleried space whose columns support a 125-foot-high dome. If you're over 18 and have photo ID, you can request and leaf through books about Freemasonry and other secret societies, the history of Washington (whether DC or George), guides to pyramids, obelisks and temples, and just about anything else that takes your fancy.

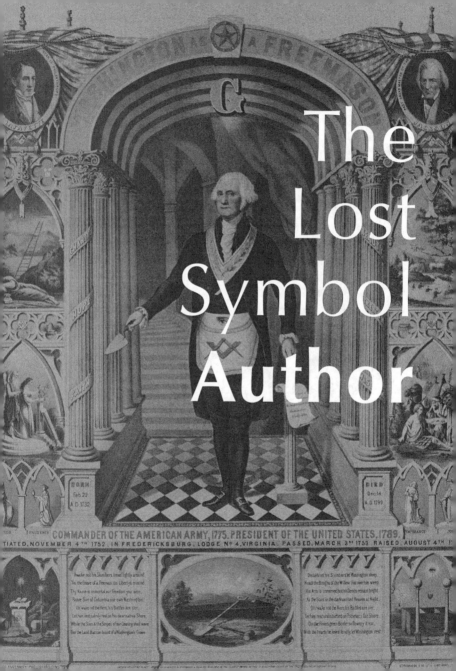

The
Lost
Symbol
Author

Dan Brown

SYMBOLS AND MYSTERIES

'At a fundamental level my interest in secret societies came from growing up in
New England, surrounded by the clandestine clubs of Ivy League universities,
the Masonic lodges of the Founding Fathers and the hidden hallways of early
government power ... In the town where I grew up, there was a Masonic lodge,
and nobody could (or would) tell me what happened behind those closed
doors. All of this secrecy captivated me as a young man.'

**DAN BROWN'S WITNESS STATEMENT TO THE
HIGH COURT IN LONDON, 2006**

Dan Brown is the world's most successful living writer.
Six and a half million copies of *The Lost Symbol* were
printed for sale in the United States, Canada, Britain and
Australia, and over a million were sold on 15 September 2009 – the
day of publication – alone. This was on the back of his previous
bestseller *The Da Vinci Code* which, since 2003, has sold well over
80 million copies in 44 languages and has reportedly earned Dan
Brown more than $250 million.

Brown's earlier books, however, had been flops. *Digital Fortress*
(1998), *Angels and Demons* (2000) and *Deception Point* (2001) sold
fewer than twenty thousand copies between them. One more book
was due under his publishing contract; if that failed too, then he

would have gone back to his quiet routine of teaching in Exeter, New Hampshire. But things turned out differently, in large measure thanks to his wife Blythe, who guided him and who was a driving force behind his success. Dan Brown's earliest inspiration, however, came from his home town itself, from his schooling there and from his early family life.

EXETER, NEW HAMPSHIRE

Dan Brown was born on 22 June 1964 in New Hampshire, the son of a mathematics teacher at Phillips Exeter Academy and a mother he has described as 'a professional sacred musician'. He was raised as an Episcopalian. Both his parents sang in the church choir; his mother has a master's degree in sacred music and is a professional church organist.

Secrets and puzzles played a large part in Brown's childhood. They had no television at home, and his parents' lives were saturated with mathematics and music – interests that fused well, Brown has said, with the family passion for anagrams, crossword puzzles and ciphers. On birthdays and at Christmas his father would create elaborate treasure hunts; instead of finding their presents under the tree, Brown and his brother and sister would find treasure maps filled with codes and clues that would lead them from room to room throughout the house – or sometimes even around the town on their bicycles – sending them from one clue to another until they finally discovered where their presents were hidden.

Exeter, a New England town of barely 14,000 people, is a few miles inland from the coast, just up the Squamscott River, named after the Native American tribe from which the Reverend John Wheelwright bought the land in 1638. Wheelwright and 135 others were refugees from the Massachusetts Bay Colony, a Puritan theocracy; they were lucky to have been exiled and not hanged, for the charge against them was heresy. On 4 July the following year they declared their settlement, named after Exeter in Devon, England, to be a self-governing and independent republic, and in 1775 it became the capital of revolutionary New Hampshire. The local Gilman family donated the first plot of land on which Phillips Exeter Academy now stands; they later contributed a Founding Father and a signatory of the United States Constitution, and one of their descendants now sits on the town's Board of Selectmen. The statue of Abraham Lincoln at Washington, DC's Lincoln Memorial was sculpted by Daniel Chester French, an Exeter native, while the architect of the Memorial itself was Henry Bacon, who designed Exeter's Swasey Pavilion. The 'Exeter Incident', which took place the year after Dan Brown was born, was one of the most widely publicized and best documented of all UFO sightings. The little town of Exeter is an American microcosm.

Dan Brown is not the first bestselling writer in his family. His father, Richard G. Brown, is the author of more than a dozen academic texts, including the bestselling *Advanced Mathematics: Precalculus with Discrete Mathematics and Data Analysis*, a standard work recommended at schools throughout the United States. Richard Brown has also received the Presidential Award for excellence in mathematics teaching.

Dan Brown and his siblings all attended the school where their father taught. Phillips Exeter Academy is the wealthiest private school in the United States and has the reputation of being the Eton of America. A string of famous Exonians have issued from the school, among them

The Phillips Exeter Academy seal bears Masonic imagery and the school motto, 'The end depends on the beginning'.

statesman Daniel Webster; Senator Jay Rockefeller; philanthropist David Rockefeller Jr; John Negroponte, director of National Intelligence; novelist Gore Vidal; Peter Benchley, author of *Jaws*; novelist and critic James Agee; beer magnate Joseph Coors; chemicals baron and industrialist Pierre S. du Pont; Drew Pearson, the 'yellow' journalist; historian Arthur Schlesinger Jr; President Franklin Pierce; Robert Lincoln, son of Abraham Lincoln; and Ulysses S. Grant Jr, son of Lincoln's general.

It may say something about Dan Brown's willingness to question the fundamental assumptions of our society that Phillips Exeter is renowned for using the Harkness method of teaching and has a student–teacher ratio of five to one. Every course at Exeter, whether calculus, literature or existential philosophy, is taught around an oval table, with the idea that learning should come as much from the interchange between students as from the teacher. The school seal is Masonic in its imagery and depicts a river, the sun and a beehive; it bears the motto, 'The end depends on the beginning'.

After finishing at Phillips Exeter, Dan Brown attended Amherst, a venerable Massachusetts liberal arts college, where he took a double major in English and Spanish and showed an interest in music composition and creative writing. He spent his junior year studying the history of art at the University of Seville and graduated from Amherst in 1986. He would later put his experience of Seville to use when writing *Digital Fortress*, his first novel.

THE MYSTERIOUS BLYTHE NEWLON

The dedication in *Angels and Demons* reads, 'For Blythe'. In *The Da Vinci Code* it reads, 'For Blythe ... again. More than ever.' And in *The Lost Symbol* it once more reads simply, 'For Blythe'. 'My wife has always been a tremendous support system,' as Dan Brown put it in his own clumsy way.

Mrs Dan Brown was born Blythe Newlon in Palmdale, a high desert town in Los Angeles County, California, in about 1952. That would make her twelve years older than her husband. But both the date and place of birth are uncertain, because almost everything about her is veiled in secrecy. Blythe does not give interviews; nor has she made public even the barest outlines of her life before 1991 when, as the influential director of artistic development at the National Academy For Songwriters in Los Angeles, she first met Dan Brown, who was clutching a portfolio of his songs and a demo CD, hoping to hit the big time as a singer-composer.

He admits he was a curious sight, describing himself as 'a fish out of water in Los Angeles'. Teaching Spanish at Beverly Hills Preparatory School by day and chasing a career in music by night, Brown lived in a low-rent apartment complex whose hallways overflowed with male models, stand-up comics, aspiring rock stars and drama queens. Blythe was twelve years older, an attractive, even glamorous woman, yet she took to him. Within no time she was making things happen. She took the unusual step, for an Academy executive, of becoming Brown's manager, and promoted his debut CD with an announcement to the trade that 'we fully expect Dan Brown will some day be included in the ranks of our [the Academy's] most successful members, talents like Billy Joel, Paul Simon and Prince'. Secretly they became lovers.

But stardom failed to call, and eventually Dan Brown concluded that 'the world isn't ready for a pale, balding geek shaking his booty; it's not a pretty picture'. But that was not before he and Blythe took a holiday, in 1993, to Tahiti, and he came across an old copy of Sydney Sheldon's *Doomsday Conspiracy* on the beach: 'I read the first page ... and then the next ... and then the next. Several hours later, I finished the book and thought, "Hey, I can do that."' A few months later, Brown took Blythe home to genteel

Exeter where he taught at Phillips Exeter Academy and in his spare time – and with Blythe's enthusiastic support – he began to write. In 1997 they married.

Dan Brown's helper and collaborator, his wife Blythe, joins the author and the French Cultural Minister at the opening dinner of the Cannes Film Festival in 2006.

Dan Brown's Books: Big Ideas

Brown's childhood love of puzzles, codes and treasure hunts made for an easy transition, as he got older, into a world where the hero undertakes a quest through a landscape of secret organizations and hidden truths. All of his books deal with secrecy in one way or another, whether in the guise of spy agencies, conspiracy theories, classified technologies or – and this was Dan Brown's biggest discovery – secret history.

Each time he has approached a new novel, Dan Brown has looked for what he calls the 'big idea'. And big for Dan Brown gets bigger all the time, now reaching out to a cosmic scale. The ideas are preposterous: in *Angels and Demons*, the Illuminati returning after two centuries to destroy the Vatican using anti-matter; in *The Da Vinci Code*, Jesus and Mary Magdalene establishing a church based on the worship of the sacred feminine, their blood-line continuing down to the present day; and in *The Lost Symbol*, our entire civilization being called into question over the separation of faith from science since the Renaissance – a denial of the divine potential of mankind.

Not many writers would have the sheer gall to take on subjects of that scale, nor could anyone expect that the Nicene Creed or Hermes Trismegistus would become the stuff of thrillers read by millions of people around the world. Yet Dan Brown has a gift for making the outrageous and arcane seem natural and accessible. Partly that is explained by the pace of his adventures, the short cliff-hanging chapters driving the reader on. But it is also that Dan Brown seems to share the deep-seated doubts and half-realized thoughts of the public mind, often on the most serious and daunting of matters, and he is able to form them into compelling and enjoyable stories. 'I think my books contain a lot of meat', he says, 'but it tastes like dessert somehow.' Here we take a look at Dan Brown's back catalogue, and then at some of his sources for *The Lost Symbol*, as well as providing our own books for further reading and a list of helpful websites.

DIGITAL FORTRESS (1998)

Dan Brown has described his moment of revelation, when he knew he could write a thriller, which came while he was reading Sydney Sheldon's *Doomsday Conspiracy* on a beach in Tahiti. The chief ingredient of a thriller is not classy writing but plot. And, as he once recounted on his website, it was the visit of two Secret Service agents to the Phillips Exeter campus, where he was then teaching, that gave him the idea for *Digital Fortress* in 1995. The agents had arrived to detain a student who had casually sent an email to a friend saying he was 'so mad at the current political situation he was ready to kill President Clinton'. The agents arrived to find out if he was just a kid mouthing off, or a potential terrorist threat.

That prompted Brown to look into how the agents got their information, and he began learning about the National Security Agency (NSA), a little-known part of the US government which, as he put it, 'functions like an enormous vacuum cleaner sucking in intelligence data from around the globe'. It was a gift of a backdrop for a thriller, and Brown neatly grafted onto it some of his knowledge of computers and cryptography. He also introduced his trademark location research – choosing the Spanish city of Seville, where he had studied, as a major setting – and a cryptographer heroine, Susan Fletcher ('a brilliant and beautiful mathematician').

ANGELS AND DEMONS (2000)

Angels and Demons was the first Robert Langdon novel – *The Da Vinci Code* was the second, and *The Lost Symbol* has now become the third. 'It was a real joy for me to write,' Brown has said of *Angels and Demons*, 'and a breakthrough in terms of finding my own style (although I can only say that with hindsight)'. He went on: 'I intend to make Robert Langdon my primary character for years to come. His expertise in symbology and iconography affords him the luxury of potentially limitless adventures in exotic locales. It was also a book in which Blythe could be more involved, as she has a great love of art and art history.'

Digital Fortress was a very clever book of its time, picking up on all kinds of aspects of the privacy debate in a new computer era. But Brown worried that it was too overtly a techno-thriller, and might be perceived as 'a computer book'. With *Angels and Demons*, he shifted terrain firmly towards conspiracy and art. The backdrop of this novel is Rome, where a series of clues propel the heroes – the 'symbology professor' Robert Langdon and a sexy, brilliant female scientist, Leonarda Vetra – through the Vatican and around the Renaissance monuments of Bernini.

A fair number of readers prefer this book to *The Da Vinci Code* because of its straightforward clash between religion and science (represented by the Swiss-based scientific research centre, CERN). The conspirators, too, are hard to resist: that hoary old bunch of anti-papists, the Illuminati. CERN, of course, is real, as is anti-matter, which falls into dodgy hands in the book.

In his mix of true facts and paranoia, and indeed the whole Illuminati setting, Brown was following on from one of the great cult conspiracy thrillers of the 1970s – the *Illuminatus!* trilogy by Robert Anton Wilson and Robert Shea. Wilson and Shea's books are (freaky) products of their age – Wilson was a big mate of Timothy Leary – but they remain entertaining reads, packed with esoteric bursts of knowledge on Sufism, futurism and counter-culture philosophy, and a lot of sex. *Angels and Demons* and *The Da Vinci Code* would appear to owe much to them.

DECEPTION POINT (2001)

Finding a US government agency more secretive even than the NSA must have proved irresistible, and Dan Brown didn't spurn the opportunities with his third thriller, *Deception Point*. The agency is the National Reconnaissance Office (NRO), which despite having a $10 billion budget and more than 10,000 employees, is unknown to most of the American taxpayers who underwrite it. The resulting novel is rather more traditional thriller fare, with real-life boys' toys technology (the Aurora 'secret' aircraft, stealth ships undetectable by radar) setting the pace. Locations, this time, include Washington and the Arctic. Robert Langdon would not have been the man for this job, so he takes time out and Intelligence analyst (and president's daughter) Rachel Sexton gets down to action.

THE DA VINCI CODE (2003)

'My hope in writing this novel was that the story would serve as a catalyst and a springboard for people to discuss the important topics of faith, religion and history,' Dan Brown said. What he set off was a firestorm that swept around the globe as *The Da Vinci Code* became the world's bestselling adult novel – a book that proved just as popular in China and Japan as in the US, Italy or Bulgaria, and long before its adaptation into a major Hollywood movie. Its appeal is three-fold: its a top-grade page-turner of a thriller, it packs in more conspiracy per page than almost any other novel you can name, and it has a backdrop of religion, art and secrecy that somehow hits a vein in our supposedly secular modern world.

Random House in the US did an amazing job of setting the initial hype, sending out an unprecedented 10,000 review copies. But it needs more than hype to create any kind of bestseller, and the appeal of *The Da Vinci Code* – which purely as a piece of thriller writing is little different from Dan Brown's three earlier books – has everything to do with its particular backdrop of art and religion, of fantasy and very deliberately stated 'fact'.

It is the 'fact', of course, that has created all the controversy: the books of rebuttal from Catholic and other Christian writers, the

MYSTERIES OF CREATION: DAN BROWN IN COURT

Dan Brown proved a revealing witness in March 2006 when he appeared at the High Court in London to defend himself against a charge of plagiarism. The plaintiffs were Michael Baigent and Richard Leigh, authors of *Holy Blood, Holy Grail* (1982). They said that Dan Brown stole their ideas when he wrote *The Da Vinci Code* (2003), in particular the great secret hidden within the code: that Jesus was married to Mary Magdalene and, after his crucifixion, that she escaped to France, where she gave birth to their child and propagated his bloodline which survives to this day. At the end of the trial the judge ruled that the plaintiff's case had failed. In using the bloodline theme, he said, 'Dan Brown has not infringed copyright'. The verdict was hardly a surprise; the judge was affirming a well established principle that there can be no copyright in ideas.

To illustrate the sources of his ideas, Dan Brown provided the court with lists of works he used for reference, not only for *The Da Vinci Code*, but also for what he called his 'work in progress'. But what – or who – led him to these sources in the first place? The surprising revelation that emerged from Dan Brown's own testimony was that the author of *The Da Vinci Code* and *The Lost Symbol* could be said to be, in a few important respects, two people. Outlining the trajectory of his career, Brown explained that he researched the techno-thrillers *Digital Fortress* (1998) and *Deception Point* (2001) almost entirely by himself, but that his wife Blythe became his 'research assistant' on *Angels and Demons* (2000) and *The Da Vinci Code*, 'This was wonderful. We were able to work together as husband and wife'.

Blythe Brown's passion for art, history and the sacred feminine is very much in evidence in both of these books, and that trajectory continued a few years later with *The Lost Symbol*, a book that can also be described as the combined effort of Dan and Blythe Brown. During *The Da Vinci Code* trial, Dan Brown told the High Court in London of his continuing research into the Knights Templar and the Freemasons, explaining that 'Blythe is helping me with the research for my new novel ... Our studies into the origins of the Christian movement and the ancient mysteries continue to this day.'

websites detailing each and every error, the guides from publishers such as ourselves. On publication, the book received predominantly enthusiastic reviews, but from the get-go, those that found the book objectionable shouted the message from the rooftops, with Christian scholars even dubbing the novel 'hate literature'.

Dan Brown arrives at London's Old Bailey court in 2006. His defence against claims of plagiarism concerning *The Da Vinci Code* was wholly successful.

Of course, a thriller that takes as its big theme the idea that the established Church is based upon a lie, and that it has distorted the true message and history of Christianity, was never going to appeal to the conventionally religious. (On his website at the time Dan Brown defined himself loosely as a Christian and 'a student of many religions'.) But the offence that the novel created was not just about religion, but about truth. Then again, one can argue that no one should expect *The Da Vinci Code* to be any more true than something by Tom Clancy or Terry Pratchett, or J.K. Rowling's world of Hogwarts, come to that. Often the book's real bits are 'fact-ish' rather than 'factual'. But what interesting territory those factish ideas occupy: the early Christian Church, the editing of the Bible, the loss of the goddess and the sacred feminine, the iconography of Leonardo da Vinci, the hidden language of codes.

A further important element behind the success of *The Da Vinci Code* was Brown's wife Blythe. She did much of the research into some of the most colourful and intriguing themes in the book, and if not the real brains, she was certainly an indispensable creative force. It was Blythe who suggested her husband introduce the bloodline theory to *The Da Vinci Code*, combining it with suppressed goddess worship and the idea of a Church of Magdalene that never was. At first he was reluctant, he has openly admitted; he thought the idea was too incredible, 'a step too far'. But eventually she convinced him. 'Blythe's female perspective was particularly helpful with *The Da Vinci Code*, which deals so heavily with concepts like the sacred feminine, goddess worship and the feminine aspect of spiritually,' he said. 'I'm not sure I had ever seen Blythe as passionate about anything as she became for the historical figure of Mary Magdalene (particularly the idea that the church had unfairly maligned her)…'

WRITING THE LOST SYMBOL

The collaboration and shared passions between Blythe and Dan Brown seems to have carried over into *The Lost Symbol*. Noetic science, intention experiments and the Ancient Mysteries all sound like subjects that Blythe could have drawn her husband into, and on which they would have worked happily together, sharing their interests. Indeed, it's interesting to note how close the sceptical Robert Langdon is drawn to the ideas of Katherine Solomon at the end of the novel, she the older woman, the harbinger of a new way of looking at the world, who sees faith and science as a whole and realizes the divinity of mankind.

The 'real' Katherine Solomon may in fact be Mrs Brown. *The Lost Symbol* begins with a dedication to Blythe, and it ends with a tribute to Blythe.

Further Reading

This is our selection of the best books on the subjects raised in *The Lost Symbol*; they are here arranged within themed categories.

FREEMASONRY

The Freemasons: A History of the World's Most Powerful Secret Society
by Jasper Ridley
Neither a Freemason nor a conspiracy theorist, Ridley is a veteran historian and biographer, who provides a balanced and thoughtful account of the Freemasons.

Revolutionary Brotherhood
by Steven C. Bullock
This traces the introduction of Freemasonry from Britain to America in the 1730s, and its role in helping to establish the new republic.

Morals and Dogma
by Albert Pike
The commentary on the degrees of the Scottish Rite written by the man who revised the rituals for the Order, and who was its greatest proponent.

The Secret Symbol
edited by Peter Blackstock
A useful and concise selection of original Masonic documents relevant to *The Lost Symbol*.

The Radical Enlightenment: Pantheists, Freemasons and Republicans
by Margaret C. Jacob
A classic work on the influence of Freemasonry on the Enlightenment.

The Origins of Freemasonry: Facts and Fictions
by Margaret C. Jacob
What factors contributed to the extraordinarily rapid spread of Freemasonry over the course of the eighteenth century, and why were so many of the era's most influential figures drawn to it? In searching for the origins of the Freemasons, Jacob discovers an early modern organization that played a historically important role while arousing a great deal of sometimes misguided public interest.

Symbols of Freemasonry
by Daniel Beresniak
Mentioned in *The Lost Symbol*, this photographic survey with text includes illustrations of a Chamber of Reflection on which Dan Brown based his description of the one to which Langdon was led in the basement of the Capitol.

Freemasonry: Symbols, Secrets, Significance
by W. Kirk MacNulty
A beautiful and lavishly illustrated portrait and history of Freemasonry.

Is It True What They Say About Freemasonry?
by Arturo de Hoyos and S. Brent Morris
Written by Thirty-third Degree Scottish Rite Freemasons, this book methodically refutes the calculated attacks against Masonry and the disparaging myths that it has suffered since its beginnings.

History

The Founding Fathers Reconsidered
by R.B. Bernstein
This concise, scholarly and eminently readable account of the men who created the United States presents them not as demigods but as imperfect human beings who achieved political greatness.

The Faiths of the Founding Fathers
by David L. Holmes
An insight into the religious beliefs of men like George Washington, Benjamin Franklin and Thomas Jefferson, and also their wives and daughters, as well as a good introduction to Deism.

The Penguin History of the USA
by Hugh Brogan
An authoritative and readable account of the entire sweep of American history. It is particularly useful for seeing the events of the revolutionary and post-revolutionary years in context.

The Templars: History and Myth
by Michael Haag
From Solomon's Temple to the Freemasons, a guide to Templar history, culture and locations.

Religion

The Age of Reason
by Thomas Paine
The famous polemic against Christianity by one of the radical Founding Fathers of the United States.

The Gnostic Gospels
by Elaine Pagels

The leading authority on the Nag Hammadi texts examines their potential significance, while resisting the lure of sensationalizing them.

The Gospel of Mary Magdalene
by Jean-Yves Leloup

A text and commentary of the Gospel of Mary Magdalene allows you to make up your own mind about the 'lost bride' of Jesus.

Lost Christianities
by Bart D. Ehrman

A scholarly, highly readable survey of the diversity of early Christianity, explaining how we came to be left with the New Testament, and ruminating over what has been lost.

Pagans and Christians
by Robin Lane Fox

A leading ancient historian, Fox lays out an absorbing and detailed portrait of the transition from paganism to Christianity up to the death of Constantine, and includes material on the Mysteries and the Hermetists.

PHILOSOPHY

History of Western Philosophy
by Bertrand Russell

Regarded by some as the greatest philsopher since Aristotle, Bertie here provides a wonderfully luminous, comprehensive and readable survey of the tradition from year dot.

The Enneads
by Plotinus

The man who invented Neoplatonism and the last great philosopher of antiquity, Plotinus blended the ideas of Plato, Aristotle and

Pythagoras into a rich synthesis which he presented in this classic of Western mysticism.

UTOPIA

The New Atlantis
by Francis Bacon
This fictional work offers an illustration of the ideal role that science should play in modern society. Its most noble institution is a great research facility called Salomon's House, which was frequently cited as a model for the Royal Society.

THE OCCULT, MYSTICISM AND SPIRITUALITY

The Secret Teachings of All Ages: An Encyclopedic Outline of Masonic, Hermetic, Qabbalistic and Rosicrucian Symbolical Philosophy
by Manly Palmer Hall
Described by Dan Brown as the core book of his research and beliefs, it is a vast compendium of the esoteric which, to extend the litany of its contents somewhat beyond its title, includes Neoplatonic philosophy, the tarot, Mystery Religions, ceremonial magic, Pythagoras, mermaids, pyramids, virgins, Freemasonry and more, plus excursions into Islam and his Bacon-as-Shakespeare thesis.

The Secret Destiny of America
by Manly Palmer Hall
Written during World War II, as America was discovering its destiny as fortress of freedom and world power, this entertaining book tells how it all began with Akhenaten ('the world's first democrat'), continued with Christopher Columbus, who was really a Greek prince, and gave rise to Francis Bacon's secret society, established in America and perpetuated by Benjamin Franklin and his friends.

Master of the Mysteries: The Life of Manly Palmer Hall
by Louis Sahagun
Written by a *Los Angeles Times* journalist who knows his way around the city and its creatures, this is an engrossing, perceptive and sympathetic book about the man himself. It also gives an insider's view of a sub-culture that continues to have a profound effect on movies, television, music, books, art and thought.

The Secret Architecture of Our Nation's Capital: The Masons and the Building of Washington DC
by David Ovason
By sufficiently bending the evidence here and there, Ovason has produced a masterpiece of occult interconnections which demonstrates a hidden cosmological symbolism in the layout of the city and its relation to the stars.

The Golden Bough
by J.G. Frazer
This famous study in myth, magic and religion provides a marvellous insight into the world described by Dan Brown as the Ancient Mysteries.

The Hiram Key
by Christopher Knight and Robert Lomas
The authors are Freemasons and they take a highly occult view of their material. The Temple of Solomon, Hiram, the ancient Egyptians, the Gnostics, Jesus, the Templars and the Freemasons are all brought together here to explain why 'the last four thousand years are never going to look the same again'.

HERMETICS

The Alchemy Reader
edited by Stanton J. Linden

An anthology of works bearing on alchemy from Plato and Aristotle through Hermes Trismegistus and the Arab writers to the English Enlightenment, concluding with Sir Isaac Newton.

Gnosis and Hermeticism from Antiquity to Modern Times
edited by Roelof van den Broek and Wouter J. Hanegraaff

Hermetism, Gnosticism, Catharism, Romanticism and the New Age, this book is an examination of what has sometimes been called the 'third component' of Western culture, the traditions that have rejected a worldview based on the primacy of rationality or of faith.

The Secret History of Hermes Trismegistus: Hermeticism from Ancient to Modern Times
by Florian Ebeling

Most useful for background on antiquity and the Middle Ages – unless you are particularly interested in the esoteric history of Germany, as that is where this book concentrates its attention once it reaches the seventeenth century.

SCIENCE AND NOETICS

The Intention Experiment
by Lynne McTaggart

This book and its author were showcased in *The Lost Symbol* and express the novel's suggestion that 'the human mind really does have the ability to affect matter'. Intention, says McTaggart, is a learned skill that has already been employed to cure illness, alter physcial processes and influence events.

Superstition: Belief in the Age of Science
by Robert L. Park
Written by a noted professor of physics, this clearly explains the scientific method and demonstrates the degree to which superstition and wishful thinking play a role in alternative health and pseudo-science practices.

Voodoo Science: The Road from Foolishness to Fraud
by Robert L. Park
The phrase voodoo science was popularized by this work, and refers to research that falls short of adhering to the scientific method. Park provides the warning signs that indicate the range of illusions, from genuine scientists deceiving themselves to outright fraud.

ART

Lives of the Artists
by Giorgio Vasari
This is one of the earliest, indeed near-contemporary, sources on Albrecht Dürer, Leonardo da Vinci and others, and has been used extensively by all subsequent biographers.

The Life and Art of Albrecht Dürer
by Erwin Panofsky
The classic academic study of Dürer presents him not only as an artist but also as a mathematician and scientific thinker.

CODES AND SYMBOLS

The Penguin Dictionary of Symbols
by Jean Chevalier and Alain Gheerbrant
A reference work used by Dan Brown, this book explores the huge variety of interpretations – spiritual and sexual, official and subversive, analytical and emotional – that different cultures have given to the fundamental symbols of humankind.

The Code Book
by Simon Singh

The story of codes, from twelfth-century Islamic cryptanalytic achievements to the most modern linguistic and computer code-cracking, illuminated by fascinating anecdotes.

Codes, Ciphers and Secret Languages
by Fred B. Wrixon

Another book used by Dan Brown, this explains all manner of technical crypto-phrases like polyalphabetic substitution cipher and so forth. Peppered with engaging anecdotes to break up the technical jargon.

Websites

The Lost Symbol has prompted enormous discussions online, while many of the subjects that it touches have an online presence in their own right. Here are a few of the more interesting sites.

THE FREEMASONS

United Grand Lodge of England
www.ugle.org.uk
The first united lodge, created in 1717 out of four London lodges.

The Grand Lodge of Scotland
www.grandlodgescotland.com

Pietre-Stones
www.freemasons-freemasonry.com
An online Freemasonry journal and archive, packed with information on a myriad of subjects.

Grand Lodge of British Columbia and Yukon
freemasonry.bcy.ca
An authoritative and comprehensive resource for Masonic research and information.

Masonic Trowel
www.themasonictrowel.com
Vast resource for things Masonic, including ancient Masonic documents.

RELIGION

Beliefnet
www.beliefnet.com
Beliefnet is a multi-faith e-community designed to help people meet their religious and spiritual needs – which it does by hosting interviews, discussions, topical articles and masses of other information on all religions. It is independent and not affiliated with any religion or spiritual movement.

Religious Tolerance
www.religioustolerance.org
A very good and inclusive site for all shades of belief from the loosest Deism to Wicca.

The Gnostic Society
www.gnosis.org
Website of the Los Angeles-based Gnostic Society, with exhaustive information on Gnosticism.

The Vatican
www.vatican.va

MYSTICISM AND THE OCCULT

Philosophical Research Society
www.prs.org
The organization founded by Manly Palmer Hall.

Manly Palmer Hall Archive
www.manlyphall.org

Hermetics Resource Site
www.hermetics.org
Includes downloadable eBooks, among them the *Greater Book of Solomon*, volume two, from which Mal'akh took his blood rituals.

SOCIETIES

The Royal Society
royalsociety.org

HISTORY

Yale University Avalon Project
avalon.law.yale.edu/subject_menus/chrono.asp
Important documents in American history in chronological order.

The Perseus Digital Library
www.perseus.tufts.edu
One of the great online resources for the ancient world and its papyri.

Internet Ancient History Sourcebook
www.fordham.edu/halsall/ancient/asbook.html
This website provides original sources for ancient history, including the Graeco-Roman world and early Christianity.

ART

The Web Gallery of Art
www.wga.hu
An excellent resource for all important artists, including a selection of Dürer's works, arranged by technique and chronologically.

Albrecht Dürer
www.albrecht-durer.org
A dedicated Dürer site, it claims to have the complete works for viewing.

CODES AND SYMBOLS

Symbols.com
www.symbols.com
Very useful for learning more about familiar symbols or discovering all sorts of symbols you never knew existed.

Elonka Dunin
elonka.com
Nola Kaye in *The Lost Symbol* is a partial anagram of Elonka, herself a cryptologist.

Elonka's Kryptos page
elonka.com/kryptos
Elonka's web page on the Kryptos sculpture at the CIA headquarters in Langley, Virginia, is the best around.

SECURITY SERVICES

CIA
www.cia.gov

NOETICS

University of Virginia: religious movements
web.archive.org/web/20060827230942/
religiousmovements.lib.virginia.edu/home.htm

Institute of Noetic Sciences
www.noetic.org
As featured in *The Lost Symbol.*

The Intention Experiment
www.theintentionexperiment.com
Set up by Lynne McTaggart, author of *The Intention Experiment*, this website is the vehicle for organizing mass experiments. Referenced along with McTaggart and her book in *The Lost Symbol*.

Princeton Engineering Anomalies Research (PEAR)
www.princeton.edu/~pear
The now defunct research organization which claimed to have proved the effect of human consciousness on the material world.

International Consciousness Research Laboratories
www.icrl.org
The organization set up by ex-PEAR people.

Quackwatch
www.quackwatch.org
A long-established and professionally supervised watchdog which surveys the practices of organizations operating in the fields of health.

DAN BROWN

Dan Brown's website
www.danbrown.com

Phillips Exeter Academy
www.exeter.edu

Exeter, New Hampshire
town.exeter.nh.us
The town's official website.

Travel

Dassault Falcon
www.dassaultfalcon.com/aircraft/2000ex
The aircraft in which Langdon flew from Boston to Washington, DC.

Beltway Limousine
www.beltwaylimousine.com
The car company that collected Robert Langdon at the airport and drove him to the Capitol.

The Washington Metro
www.wmata.com
For a quick escape across town.

George Washington

The George Washington Papers
gwpapers.virginia.edu
The private papers of the first president of the United States.

Mount Vernon
www.mountvernon.org
George Washington's private home outside Washington, DC.

Washington DC

Architect of the Capitol
www.aoc.gov
This is the position held down by Warren Bellamy in *The Lost Symbol*.

Library of Congress
www.loc.gov
The Jefferson Building and the John Adams Building were the scenes of Langdon's escape from the Capitol Building.

Washington National Cathedral
www.nationalcathedral.org
The Episcopalian sanctuary to which Langdon and Katherine escaped after leaving the Library of Congress.

Smithsonian Institution
www.si.edu
The famous institution of which Peter Solomon is the head.

National Gallery of Art
www.nga.gov/
This prestigious gallery possesses a number of Dürer's works including a version of *Melencolia I*.

The Washington Monument
www.nps.gov/wamo
The Ancient Mysteries lie below it.

Washington, DC architecture
american-architecture.info/USA/USA-Washington/DC.htm
A website describing the sites from an architectural point of view.

Supreme Council of the Scottish Rite, Southern Jurisdiction
www.scottishrite.org
Mal'akh comes here to be raised to the Thirty-third Degree, and returns here later to be sacrificed by his father.

George Washington Masonic Memorial
www.gwmemorial.org
Langdon and Katherine gave the CIA the slip by pretending to be headed here, but they took the Metro in the opposite direction.

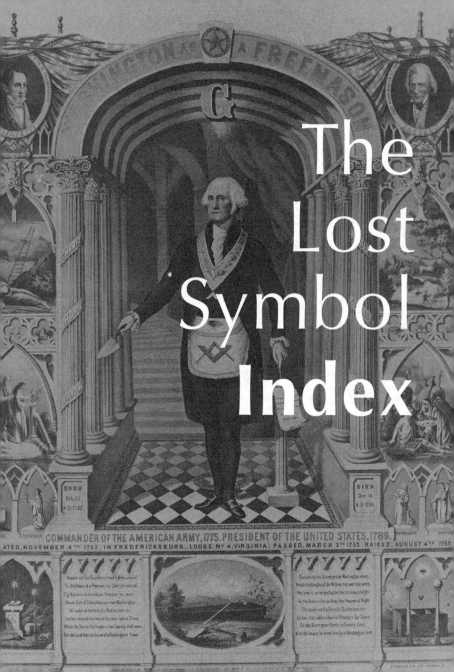

The
Lost
Symbol
Index

Index

INDEX

PHOTOGRAPHIC CREDITS

The Publishers have made every effort to identify correctly the rights holders in respect of the images featured in this book. If despite these efforts any attribution is absent or incorrect, the Publishers will correct this error once it has been brought to their attention on a subsequent reprint.

Alamy: © Rob Crandall/Alamy 29; © Geoffrey Morgan/Alamy 87; Almay 10; © William S. Kuta/Alamy 171; © Pat & Chuck Blackley/Alamy 176; © Photo Art Collection (PAC)/Alamy 191

Bridgeman Art Library: Private Collection/The Bridgeman Art Library 25; Bibliotheque Nationale, Paris, France/Archives Charmet/The Bridgeman Art Library 45

Corbis: © Craig Aurness/CORBIS 13; © Catherine Karnow/CORBIS 21; © Bettmann/CORBIS 42, 73; © Kim Kulish/Corbis 80; © Burstein Collection/ CORBIS 113; © Bettmann/CORBIS 147, 188; © Cameron Davidson/Corbis 195; © Blaine Harrington III/Corbis 214–15; © Stephane Cardinale/People Avenue/Corbis 224; © Lindsey Parnaby/epa/Corbis 230

DK Images/Rough Guides: © Kim Sayer Dorling Kindersley 18, 182, 205; DK Images 38, 90, 91, 172; Angus Osborn © Rough Guides 174, 182, 197, 200, 208

Getty Images: Getty Images 17; De Agostini/Getty Images 28; Time & Life Pictures/Getty Images 52; AFP/Getty Images 172

Library of Congress: 34, 125, 142; William Strickland 54; Brady-Handy Photograph Collection 66; Harris & Ewing Collection 155

Mary Evans Picture Library: 59, 70

Philosphical Research Society: Courtesy of the Philosophical Research Society, Inc., www.prs.org

Wikipedia: 97